Amaro Cavalcanti

The Brasilian Language and its Agglutination

Amaro Cavalcanti

The Brasilian Language and its Agglutination

ISBN/EAN: 9783743333642

Manufactured in Europe, USA, Canada, Australia, Japa

Cover: Foto ©ninafisch / pixelio.de

Manufactured and distributed by brebook publishing software
(www.brebook.com)

Amaro Cavalcanti

The Brasilian Language and its Agglutination

PREFACE

The principal object of the present elementary book is: (1) to verify if several opinions suggested by philologists and linguists, as the peculiar characteristics of the so-called « agglutinative languages » are, indeed, found in the Brazilian language ;— (2) to contribute, by some informations on the grammatical elements and processes of this language, for the progress of *Comparative Grammar*.

« We use the terms « Brazilian language », as embracing the several dialects spoken in Brasil by the savage tribes, since the discovery of the country.

Among those dialects, the *Guarany* and the *Tupy* are the most important. They hold the same close relation, as is found between *High and Low German*. — *Guarany* was spoken, principally, in the South-part of Brazil, and *Tupy,* along the coast, at the time of the discovery, and now, in the central parts of some provinces of the North, especially, in Pará, Amazonas and in the border-territories.

«— The language of cultivated people, as it is known, is the Portuguese».

Rio de Janeiro, December, 2, 1883.

KEY

TO THE PRONUNCIATION AND READING

VOWELS

a, e, i, o, u, (unmarked) have *short sounds*, sometimes scarcely perceptible in ending syllables.

∧ (upon vowel) markes *long sound*.
˛ (» ») « *broad sound*.
∪ (upon u) « a **guttural sound**, like the Greek υ.
∼ (upon any vowel) markes **nasal sound**:— *am, em, im, om, um*.
❜ markes stress of voice (accent) upon certain syllables of words.

CONSONANTS AND DIPTHONGAL SOUNDS
"will be indicated afterwards"

PRINCIPAL ABREVIATIONS USED:

Lat	Latin.
Ger	German.
Eng.	English.
It	Italian.
Fr.	French.
Sp.	Spanish.
Port.	Portuguese.
Br.	Brasilian.

Sing.	Singular.
Pl.	Plural.
Pers.	Person.
Prep.	Preposition.
Adv.	Adverb.
Conj.	Conjunction.
Interj	Interjection.
Nom.	Nominative case.
Gen.	Genitive case.
Dat.	Dative case.
Acc.	Accusative.
Abl.	Ablative.
i e.	*Id est* (that is).
Adj	Adjective.
Pron.	Pronoun.
Poss.	Possessive.
Lang.	Language.
Pref.	Preffix.
Sf.	Suffix.
rad.	radical.
cf.	*confer* (compare).
lit.	literally.
ex:	for example.
on.	onomatopaic.

CHAPTER I

CLASSIFICATION OF LANGUAGES

1. — Glottology divides the numerous languages of the World, according to the peculiarities of their grammatical structure, into three classes: (1) Monosyllabic or Isolating; (2) Agglutinative; (3) Inflectional or Polysyllabic.

These terms also represent three periods in the growth of languages, that is to say, that language, as an organism, may pass through three stages, as follows: [1]

---

[1] Dr. R. Morris, *English Accidence*, pag. 2.

(I)

— *The monosyllabic period,* in which roots are used, as words, without any change of form.

In this stage there are no prefixes or suffixes, and no formally distinguished parts of speech.

The *Chinese* is the best example of a language in the isolating or monosyllabic stage.

« Every word in *Chinese* is monosyllabic; and the same word, without any change of form, may be used, as a *noun,* a *verb,* an *adjective,* an *adverb* or a *particle.* Thus, *ta,* according to its position in a sentence, may mean great, greatness, to grow, very much, very. »

« We cannot in *Chinese* (as in Latin) derive from *ferrum,* iron, a new substantive *ferrarius,* a man who works in iron, a blacksmith; *ferraria,* an iron-mine; and again, *ferrariarius,* a man who works in an iron-mine; all this is possible only in an inflected language. » [2]

In the languages of this last kind, the various relations of thought are declared by means of certain *formative elements* (suffixes and inflec-

---

[2] Dr. R. Morris, *English Accidence,* pag. 2.

tions) joined to *root* or to *thême*, as we see in the examples above.

In *Chinese,* on the contrary, such relations are declared by the simple disposition of words in the sentence. Thus, *ngò tà mi,* means « I strike thee, » and *mi tà ngò* means, on the contrary, « thou strikest me ; » *fu,* father, *mu,* mother, and *fu-mu,* parents (Fr. *parents); shi,* ten, *eül,* two, and *eül-shi,* twenty; i. e: two ten ; *gin,* a man, *kiai,* many, (collection, assembly, etc.), *gin-kiai,* men ; *kûô,* empire, *cung,* middle (or midst), *kûô-cung,* in the empire ; i. e:—the word, *cung,* joined to a noun, converts it into the *locative case* of the Indo-European languages. (³)

(2)

2.— *The agglutinative period.* — In this stage two unaltered, or scarcely modified roots are joined together to form words; in these *compounds* one root becomes subordinate to the other, and so loses its independence: cf:—*man-*

(³) Max. Müller, *Science of Language.*

kind, heir-loom, war-like, which are agglutinative compounds.

So long as words keep their radical meaning, the language remains in its first period, *that of roots*.

But, since certain words, by losing their original or etymological import, have become mere signs of *derivation,* the language has reached to its second period, *that of desinences,* (terminations of word). ([4])

The greatest portion of the languages, spoken in the World, remain in this second stage; and all of them form the so-called Turanian-group, which, in the present condition of science, might give the explanation of most important problems, if it were better studied by the living philologists.

According to Prof. Townsend, this group of tongues is found, first and last, to have ranged from Norway almost to Behring's Straits; ([5]) and according to the opinion of Mr. Müller, it embraces two great divisions: that of the North that of the South.

([4]) Max. Mullor, *Science of Language, cit.*

([5]) L. T. Townsend (Prof. in Boston Wulversity) — *The Art of Speech.*

The former, called sometimes the *Ural-altaic*, is again divided into five sections: the languages of the *Tonguses*, the *Mongols*, the *Turks*, the *Finns*, the *Samoyeds*.

The latter, which occupies the South-part of Asia, is also divided into four sections : the *Tamul*, the dialects of *Tibet* and *Bhotan*, the dialects of *Siam* and those of *Malaca* and *Polynesia*.

With the group of the *agglutinative languages* are classed the *African* tongues, so-called *atonic*, the words of which are mostly formed by means of prefixes, a characteristic, that distinguishes them from the *Ural-altaic* tongues, which, as a rule, do not admit of the root of a word occupying the second place.

Still there must be considered, as belonging to the same *agglutinative group*, the numerous dialects or tongues of America ; and among these, those, spoken by Brasilian savages, present undoubtedly all the *supposed essential characteristics* of an *agglutinative language*, as we hope to prove beyond contest by our further illustrations.

3.— It is, certainly, too difficult for the linguist to establish a distinct and uniform classification out of the speeches of those multitudes of scattered races and tribes; but it is just this want of uniformity in their grammatical forms or in their usages and applications, which constitutes one of the fundamental reasons of *this group*.

« They are speeches of nomadic people and of savages, and only, by this characteristic, they des tinguish themselves from the *Aryan and Semitic* languages. In these two families of tongues, « *Aryan* and *Semitic* » the majority of words and their grammatical forms were produced, at once, for all of them, by the creative force of one generation; and it would be very difficult to abandon them, though their primitive clearness had been obscured by further phonetic alterations.

« The transmission of a language in such conditions would be only possible among people, whose history flows, as a large river, and among whom religion, laws and poetry serve, like dams, to bound the current of speech.

« But we know, that among nomadic people there was never established a true nucleus of political, social and literary institutions.

Their, so-called, empires were no sooner founded, than they were scattered, like sand-clouds in the desert: — almost no laws, legends, stories and songs have survived the generation, that saw them rise (⁶).

(3)

4. — *The inflectional period.* In this stage roots are modified by prefixes or suffixes, which were once independent words.

In agglutinative languages the union of words, says Dr. R. Morris, may be compared to mechanical compounds, in inflective languages to chemical compounds.

« I call *period of flections,* adds Prof. M. Müller, that one, in which roots are blended in such a way, that none of them keeps a genuine and total independence, as it is found in the Aryan and Semitic families.

« The first period does not admit of phonetic alteration, at all.

« The second period does not admit of such alteration in the principal root, but admits of it in the secondary or demonstrative elements.

« The third period admits of phonetic altera-

(⁶) Mr. Muller, *w. cit.*

tion, both in the principal root and in the desinences *(flections)*. »

In most living languages we find traces of all these processes, and thus are enabled to see how one stage leads gradually to another.

Take, for example, the following.

ENGLISH

He is like God, = *monosyllabic*
He is God-like, = *agglutinative*. (*)
He is God-ly, = *inflectional*.

GERMAN

Mann ist frei, = *monosyllabic*
Er ist *frei-mann*, = *agglutinative*
Er ist frei-*mannes* (gen.), = *inflectional*.

By carefully inquiring, we should be able to discover similar instances in the Romance-languages, although not so frequently, in relation to the *monosyllabic and agglutinative* forms.

5. — The very learned American linguist, Prof. Whitney, in his important book — « Life

---

(*) Dr. Morris, book cit. — pag. 3.

and Growth of language,» discussing on the subject-matter, says, as follows:

« Proceeding by analogy and taking, as a starting point, the Indo-European languages, we can state,—that what the remaining languages of the World may contain about the matter of *flections* and of *formative instruments*, has all been elaborated, as in these languages, from the mass of a rude vocabulary, formed with entirely concrete words, which constitutes the primitive period of languages.

« If, however, it were possible to demonstrate the existence of languages,—which were brought forth at once, as *inflectional;* then, this opinion should be renounced. But very rigorous proofs would be required for making good such a demonstration.

« Language is an instrument, and the *law of the simplicity of beginnings* is applied to languages, as it is to any other thing.

Each root must have begun by containing, (as it is still noted, now-adays, in certain monosyllables under the character of interjections,) an affirmation, an idea, a question, an order, etc.,— and the *tone* and the *gesture* or the *circumstances* would complete their signification. »

THE STUDY OF LANGUAGE

6. — Among all languages, the *Aryan or Indo-European* family is the only one, which has been well studied by linguists, in the present condition of our knowledge of the matter. This preference of studies, which has brought forth the best results to science, is quite justified by the capital reason, that in that family of languages are found the richest scientific and literary monuments of the three classical languages of mankind,—*Sanskrit, Greek,* and *Latin.*

«In relation to the study of the other languages, «Semitic, monosyllabic and agglutinative » we may affirm, that our scientific knowledge about it is yet entirely unsatisfactory, and does not enable the philologist to profer a conscientious decision on the very important problem of their reciprocal relations among themselves, and to the *Aryan* family.

« Leaving aside the group of *isolating languages*, represented by the Chinese and by the Indo-Chinese, who lead their lives, separately from other people; it is true, that the greatest ignorance prevails, relating to the *agglutinative tongues*, although these be spoken by innumerable nations in the five parts of the World.

The only circumstance, which may somewhat excuse such a fault, is the lack of literary monuments, that provoke the curiosity and wish to know them.

7.— By reading, sometimes, the best authors on the subject, we have found frequent hypotheses, the ones, suggested by mere logical inductions, the others, based on informations, not well established, and most of them, wanting of every scientific *criterium*. And although it may seem strange to some, these facts, which came under our observation, have constituted for us the primary motive for writing the present elementary book.

In comparing the grammatical forms and the logical processes of some other languages, with the usages and manners of the common speech of Brasilian savages; we arrived at the well established conclusion, that in the uncultivated language of these people, not only are there found grammatical forms, used regularly and in accordance with logical principles; but also, that the same language offers an evident confirmation of the various hypotheses, which have been advanced by philologists, when intending to characterize the *agglutinative family*.

We have not yet any settled fact, relating to the ethnographic origin of the Brasilian savages, nor to the particular point of their primitive or derived speech. No accurate inquiry or successful investigation exists on this very important matter.

It is, however, a fact of the easiest intuition, that an immense result would issue for history and science, if it were possible to prove, in a satisfactory way : — « from what country these millions of individuals who came to live in America emigrated ; — in what century this great event happened ; — and what speech, what religion, what degree of civilisation they have brought with them to the lands of their new abodes. »

For want of these important *data*, the only way to obtain some regular information, relating to the language of our savage tribes, is, undoubtedly, to study and analyse their forms and processes in the state and conditions, in which they have come to our knowledge and actual observation. *As a guide,* or as auxiliary instruments, to such work, we have nothing more, than those books of prayer or instruction, prepared by missionaries, about four ou five generations ago, which have become in a great part antiquated.

Words and their uses arise to meet some wants of the time; they disappear, when no longer needed.

From all these circumstances it results, that this elementary work will be framed from no abundant materials; and, therefore, not only it will be of more difficult execution, but also, as a natural consequence, not entirely satisfactory.

Notwithstanding, we hope to be able to avoid every error in the statement of principles and their dependent facts.

THE BRASILIAN LANGUAGE AND ITS POSITION

8. — The Brazilian language exhibits itself under an aspect, quite uncultivated. The people, who speak it, do not possess, at the best, the knowledge of the aphabetic signs; they are, simply, *savages,* the most complete type of human ignorance.

Nevertheless, by studying all the organism or

the structure of such savage speech, and making rigorous analysis of its forms, used regularly in the expression of thoughts; it results, to evidence, that it has passed the monosyllabic period, and has kept itself, long since, in the agglutinative stage, which is owing, perhaps, to the want of indispensable culture, which enables it to reach the richest stage of a language,— *that of inflection*.

It is a fact sufficiently proved by experience and by the existing writings on the subject, that the morphology and the syntax of the Brazilian language have been kept unaltered, since the discovery of the country up to the present days. The grammatical elements and forms in usage, which, in this respect, were soon noted by the missionaries, at the time of their catechising among the savage tribes, so far back as the $16°$ century, are still almost identical with these, which may be observed in the speech of the remaining people of the same race.

It is certain, that the greatest alteration is noted in its phonetic forms, and, consequently, in its vocabulary which is, now, very different from that of the times of the discovery and the conquest of the country.

Besides the natural phonological laws, which govern the frequent changes of every vocable;

with respect to Brazilian savage people, there occurred another circumstance, that ought to influence and to increase this result, that is :— that these people were, in general, composed of nomadic tribes; and it is easy to imagine, — how gradually from differences of climate and of natural scenery,—from differences in the various objects of perception, each day renewed, whatever they might be, there should result differences of *speech, especially with respect to the words, already in usage.*

9.—As a point, deserving especial remark, we must declare, now, that in various instances of usages of the Brazilian speech, there are still found certain processes, pertaining to the *isolating period,* — as for example,— the invariable place of words in a sentence, which, as it is known, constitutes almost the entire grammar of the languages of this kind. But this circumstance, though important, is not sufficient to decide against our opinion, given before; because in Brazilian tongues are found also all the other characteristics, which are, generally, required in the very *agglutinative languages.*

— « Agglutination, writes Mr. Müller, does not mean only, that in the grammar pronouns are, so to say, glued to verbs in order to form the conjugation, or prepositions to substantives to form the declension; — because it would not be a distinct character of nomadic tongues, only, for both in Sanskrit and Hebrew the conjugation and the declension were originally constituted, according to the same principles.

But that which distinguishes the *Turanian languages* (agglutinative) is, that the words, which form their conjugation and declension, are always susceptible of easy decomposition; and although in many cases the terminations keep their modificative value, as independent words, yet one sees, that these are *modificative* syllables, quite distinguished from the *roots*, to which they are joined. (⁷)

— The hypotheses advanced by the very learned linguist, M. Müller, are entirely identical with those, which Prof. Whitney has verified in the *Scythic tongues*, that he considered, as a complete type of the *agglutinative family*.

« By this term, adds Whitney, one means to say, that the elements of several origins, which compose the *Scythic* words and their forms are

---

(⁷) *Science of lang.* cit.

less blended, less closely aggregated; and that, therefore, they keep themselves more independent, than in the *Indo-European languages*.

« The *root*, as a rule, remains invariable in all derived words, and each *suffix* also keeps its form and invariable application:— and from this results, on the one side, great regularity of forms, on the other, great complication.

For instance, in Turkish, *lar(*or *ler)* is the form of the plural;—to it are joined terminations or *particle-suffixes*, — which form the cases of the singular number, and there may still be inserted pronominal elements, indicative of possession; thus: — *ev,* house, *ev-den,* of a house; *ev-üm-den,* of my house;— *ev-ler,* houses; *ev-ler-üm-den,* of my houses.

« The verb presents an analogical and still more striking example. — There are a few modifying elements, that may be inserted, either isolated, or grouped in different ways, between the root and the terminations, to express *passivity, reflexion, reciprocity, causality, negation, impossibility,* etc.

« The distinction between verbs and nouns is not quite so original and fundamental, as in the Indo-European languages. The words used, as verbs, are scarcely distinguished from nouns, that are used *predicatively,* on their appearing combined with subjects or possessive pronouns.

« The *Scythic* adjective is deprived of flection, like the English adjective; and there is the same lack of gender in nouns and pronouns, as in *Persian*.

« Words, which indicate relations, and conjunctions, are almost entirely unknown; the combination of the terms of a sentence is made, as is natural, «wherein verbs are not quite distinguished,» by means of *declensions* and *verbal nouns*.» ([8])

— Except this last observation, relative to the words, which express *relations* and *conjunctions,* which are very numerous in Brazilian languages; we think, we are enabled to affirm, that in this speech are clearly and, perhaps, better realised all the characteristics, that Mr. Whitney has reputed essential to every *agglutinative language.*

From the clearly made analysis and the explanations, which will be given in the following chapters, we hope, the truth of our proposition will be firmly established.

([8]) Life & Growth of Lang. cit.

CHAPTER II

PHONETIC PRINCIPLES

10.—A fact, generally noted by linguists, is —the rapidity or facility, with which the dialects and tongues of people, deprived of literary monuments, are altered or changed.

Literature serves, so to say, as the standard, after which the spoken language is modelled in order to be preserved in its integrity.

—In relation to the savage tribes of Brasil, the frequent change of their vocabulary was one of the leading circumstances, which were noted by the catechising missionaries, who, very often, expressed their admiration at the fact, that a dialect had undergone, within a short time, after it was knwon, so many alterations, as to become quite a different one.

They have observed, that the names of the most common objects themselves, as, for instance, — *father, son, etc,* were, sometimes, so much altered by pronunciation, that they formed different words, and, sometimes, were replaced by synonyms of remote relation.

All this was, indeed, very natural.

« One must not, says W. von Humboldt, consider a language, as a dead product formed, once for all: it is an animate being and ever creative. Human thought elaborates itself with the progress of intelligence; and language is a manifestation of this thought.

« An idiom cannot, therefore, remain stationary.

« It changes, it develops, it grows up, it fortifies itself, it becomes old, and it reaches decrepitude. »

11. — According to these principles, it is reasonable to admit, that there must be many words, used among each class of the Brasilian nomadic tribes, which were not understood by the rest.

Besides this, simpler causes, such, for instance, as result from the use of synonymous terms, would be sufficient to produce radical *word-changes*.

We know that, when there are several equivalent terms in a language to express the same idea or object, it is very common, that the dialects, — issuing from this language, select diversely, among such equivalent terms, and, as a rule, one of these becomes the prevailing one in one dialect, another in another, to the neglect and loss of all, but the one selected. (¹)

— We insist on this point, though sufficiently proved by constant observation, as the fundamental reason, or the cause, that most contributed to the formation of the numerous dialects, which composed the Brasilian speech, at the time of the discovery and conquest of the country.

According to our humble opinion, all Brasilian tribes spoke tongues of one general family, although much altered by frequent phonetic changes, owing, principally, to the above-mentioned causes.

Among the leading reasons, which enable us to emit such a proposition on the nature of Brasilian tongues, there exists one, that, as we think, should be regarded, as of the most legitimate inference, viz: — that in all Brasilian dialects, of which there are grammars and vocabularies, some of which were composed, since the colonial period, we find the greatest agreement in gram-

---

(¹) Townsond, book cit.

matical forms. Especially, with respect to the morphological and syntactical processes, their identity is an evident fact, beyond all possible contest.

SOUNDS AND LETTERS

12. — The letters of the *Latin alphabet,* which may be used to represent the phonetic elements of the Brasilian language, are the following :

a, b, d, e, g, h, i, k, (= c, q,) m, n, o, p, r, s, (= ç,) t, u, x, y. ([2])

« The letters — f, j, l, v, z — find no employment in this lang. »

When we have well understood and compared certain little discordances, which are found in the authors, most of them owing to diversity of characters, chosen, as representatives of sound, for instance, the one having used the *Spanish* alphabet, the other the *German,* another the

---

([1]) We call *Latin alphabet* — in the state, wherein it passed to the Romance languages.

Portuguese, and yet another, the *French* and so on ;—we can, rightly affirm, that the alphabetic characters, above indicated, have been, as a rule, considered sufficient and quite apropriate to the phonetic usages of the Brasilian language. ([3])

Consonants

13.— We preferred this letter—*s,* instead of —*c* before *e, i,* and *ç,* which have been adopted by some writers.

It is observed, that the *hissing* of *s* is contrary to the savage's pronunciation. But we cannot admit of such a reason, as a good one; because it cannot be denied, that the syllables *ça, ce, ci,* have the same phonetic value, as, *sa, se, si,* in Latin pronunciation.

Moreover, the *s* has in itself the advantage of replacing the two characters— *ç, c,* (the latter before *e, i*), and, therefore, it will be used in this book, as representative of the sound *c,* in the word *city.*

([3]) *Cf:*— A. G. Dias, *Dict. of Tupy Lang* ; Montoya, *Arte, Vocabulary* and *Treasury of Guarany Lang* ; Figueira, *Gram. of Brasil. Lang* ; Dr. Couto Magalhães, *The Savage;* Mamiani, *Gram. of the Kiriri Lang.,* etc. etc.

G g, is only used, with a hard sound, before *a, o, u,* as in the word—*garden.* This letter keeps the same sound in ending syllables, and sometimes becomes nasal, as we shall see hereafter.

H h, before a vowel, is the sign of a soft aspiration.

R r, has always a very soft sound, something like the *r* in the French word—*j'aimerai,* I will love.

X x, is pronounced, like *sh* in the word *she,* or the German *sch,* in the word *schaf,* sheep.

Y y, is used to represent a sound, like *ii,* as the *i* consonant *in Italian,* or the German *j* in the words—*Jagd, Jäger, Jeder.*

Nh. This compound sound is perfectly equivalent to the French *gn* in the word *mignon,* delicate.

« The other *consonants,* respecting which we do not make any observation, will be pronounced, as their correspondent ones in the English alphabet. »

Ba, be, bo.— These syllables, in some words, are nasal, that is, they are pronounced, as if they had an *m* before :=*mba, mbe, mbo.*

Na, ne, ni, no—are, also, pronounced with

as strong a nasal sound, as if they had a *d* between the consonant and the vowel :=*nda, nde, ndi, ndo.*

Vowels

A

14.— *a* (unmarked) has the brief sound of the Portuguese *a* in the preposition *para* = to and for, or of the final *a* in the word— *America*; ex: *marika,* the belly. In final syllables, this short sound sometimes becomes almost undistinguishable, as :— *menára,* to marry.

â has a long sound, as the *a* of the Portuguese word *fado,* fate, or of the *a* in *father*; ex:— *tauâ,* the town.

à has a *broad* sound, almost like two *aa*; ex: —*parà,* the sea (or a large river); *abà,* creature.

ã has, finally, a nasal sound, like the Portuguese compound *am*; ex:—*Tupã, God ; kunhã,* woman.

E

e (unmarked) has a brief sound, sometimes almost undistinguishable, like the *e* in the word *some*; ex: *petima,* tabaco ; *moâme,* to arm.

é has the long sound of the *French é* in the word *eté*, the summer; ex: *iké*, here, *keté*, to or for (prep.)

è has a sound, like the first *è* in the word *where*; ex: *ipéka*, the goose; — *etè*, much (excellent).

ẽ has, finally, a nasal sound, as the Portuguese compound *em*; ex:—*hẽhẽ*, yes.

I

i (unmarked) has a brief sound as in the word *ill*; ex: *ibdk*, heaven.

ĩ has the nasal sound of the Portuguese compound *in*, ex:—*mirĩ*, small.

[See *y*, before.]

O

o (unmarked) has the brief sound of the Portuguese *o* in final syllables, almost undistinguishable, as in the verb—*amo*, I love; ex: *ixebo*, to me; — *yo* (particle, which expresses the reciprocal action of the verb.)

ô has a long sound, almost—*u*, as in the verb to *go,* or rather in to *prove;* ex: *mô* (particle, formative of active verbs); *pô,* the hand.

ò has a sound, like the diphthong *aw* in the word—*law;* ex: *sòkò,* Brasilian bird; *ikò,* to *be,* (=Port. estar).

õ has, finally, a nasal sound, as the Port. compound—*on;* ex:—*mõdá,* to steal.

U

u (unmarked) has a short sound, like *u* in *full;* ex: *mu,* brother.

û has a long sound, something like *oo* in *too* (adv.) ex: *tasûba,* fever.

ŭ has a very peculiar sound, something like the German *ü,* or *rather* the Greek ʋ*;* ex: *mŭra,* wood.

« This sound of *ŭ* is, generally, represented by the grammarians of the Brasilian language by *y,* which they have called *the full i.* »

ũ has, finally, a nasal sound, like the Port. compound— *um;* ex: *pitũna,* night (dark or black.)

Diphthongs

15.—The principal diphthongs of the Bras. lang. are the following : —

Ai

It sounds, like the German diphthong *ai* in *Kaiser*, the emperor ; ex : *mairi*, city.

Au

It sounds like *ow* in the adverb—*now;* ex: *auá*, who?

Ei

It sounds, just like the alphabetic sound of *a*, in the word *fate;* ex:—*eima*, spindle.

Eu

It has the sound of the Portuguese diphthong *éo* in the words *céo*, heaven ; *véo*, veil ; ex : *monbéu*, to confess.

Oi

It has the sound of the Italian *oi* in the pronouns *noi*, we; *voi*, you ; ex : *mokoi*, two.

Ui

It has the sound, which results from the two short vowels *u* and *i*, being pronounced together ; ex : *piü*, slight or delicate.

[We find in Brazilian words other examples of two or even three successive vowels; but they are, in general, pronounced distinctly, and, so, do not make diphthongs or triphthongs properly so-called.]

TABLE OF THE ALPHABETIC SOUNDS
Consonants

	Sharp	Flat	Aspirate	Nasal	Trilled
Gutturals.	$K=(c, q)$	G	H	Ng, Nh	
Palatals..	....	....	Y, X	....	R
Dentals ..	D	T	S	N, Nd	
Labials ..	B	P	....	M, Mb	

Volwels

a	â	à	ã (*)
e	ế	è̇	ẽ
i	....	....	ĩ
o	ô	ò	õ
u	û	ŭ	ũ

(*) [See Key to the pronunciation and reading, ...]

PHONETIC ALTERATIONS

16.—It is to be recollected, that the Brasilian language is the speech of savage tribes, destitute of every notion of letters and of their representative value in pronunciation; and, therefore, it is unnecessary to premise, that we are not able to state all the rules, which govern the phonetic developments of their language. Yet, by making a patient analysis of its vocabularies, grammars and other literary informations we could obtain; we have come to ascertain in this language some of the general principles, which are of frequent application in its *phonetics*.

For instance, although it is a language spoken by savage people, as we said, it is liable to general laws, which produce *phonetic alterations;* viz : *greater facility* of *pronunciation,* and *better harmony of sounds*: — the former, a physiological principle; — the latter, a euphonical principle.

From these two principles results, that *harder sounds* pass successively into *softer,* and *unpleasing sounds* become *sonorous* or *euphonical*.

So far as we can see in the matter, in the phonetic alterations of Brasilian languages, prevail the following rules :

PERMUTATION OF SOUNDS

(a)

17.— The savage tribes of Brasil very often confound certain consonants in pronunciation, especially, when they belong to the same organ, as *p, m* and *b; n,* and *d; r, s* and *t*.

It is also necessary to note, that the most frequent changes take place in the processes of agglutination *(composition and derivation by*

prefixes, and suffixes, or juxta-position);
ex: *Tápè = Taba*, town, + *pè*, = supè, (prep.)
to, — to the town ; — *moraukepé = morauke*,
work, labor, + *pè = yepè*, one or the first, —
Monday, that is, the first working-day.

(e)

18. — When the pronouns of the first and second persons sing.— xe = *se*, *(I* and my*)* ;— *nè = re,* (thou and thy) — are followed by some word beginning with *t*, this is changed into *r*; ex: —*tatá*, fire, — *se* or *xe-ratá*, my fire ; *túba*, father, *ne-ruba*, thy father.

(1)

19. — If the possessive pronoun *i*, his, her and whose, etc., is followed by a word, beginning with *s*, this is changed into *x*; ex: *Siyra*, aunt, —*i-xiyra*, his or her aunt; *Siy*, mother,— *i-xiy*, her or his mother ; *só*, to go, — *i-xó*, his going ; *sui*, of, —*i-xui*, of him or of her ; *supè*, to, — i-*xupè*, to him, etc.

(o)

20.— When, however, the *s* is preceded by another vowel of different sound, it is frequently changed into *r*, ex: *Sáua*, hair, — *se-ráua*, my hair; — *ré-rdua*, thy hair; — *saisú*, to love, — *Tupã raisú*, to love God.

(u)

Nasal sounds are very frequent in Brasilian speech; and, as a general rule, when a preceding vowel is nasal, the following must also be nasal; ex:

Nahã, that, *amô*, other; — *nahã-ãmô*, that other. As it is seen, the *a* of *amô* becomes *nasal*, because of the *ã* of *nahã*.

SUPPRESSION AND ADDITION OF LETTERS

(1)

21.— *Aphæresis*. Sounds (letters) are dropt, very frequently, in the beginning of words. — «*Accent plays an important part in these changes; unaccented syllables, which precede the accented one, are the most liable to drop off.*»

Take, for example, the following :

Urápára, bow,=*mŭrápára;*—«*mŭrá,* (wood) + *pára,* to bow, bowed or crooked);—*pè,* (prep. corresponding to the dative and locative case,)= *supè,* in, or to; *nè* or *rè* (pron.) = *inè* or *irè,* thou or thy;—*xè* (pron.)= *ixè,* I or my, etc. etc.

22.— *Syncope.* There also are found various instances of letters dropt in the body of words, most usually in the agglutination of roots with suffixes or prefixes; ex : *tāuasú,* a hog, = *tanhāudsú (tanha,* tooth + *uasú,* long) ; *koatia-sába,* painting, = *koatiára,* + *sába; kameri-kára,* a kneader, = *kamerike* + *ára* [38, 39].

23.— *Apócope.* The suppression of letters in the end of words is most generally noted in unaccented syllables; ex : *akán,* the head , = *akánga;*—*men(d)ár,* to marry, = *mendára;*— *pótár,* to wish, = *pótare;* etc. etc.

(2)

24.—*Prothesis.* Letters, as a rule, are added at the beginning of a word, to produce a nasal or more euphonical sound; ex : — *mbaè,* thing, =*baè;*—*ikatù-retè,* very good, = *katù,* good + *etè,* much or very; *imŭra,* wood, = *mŭra ;* — *epy̆a,* the heart, = *py̆a;*— *epô,* the hand, = *pô.*

25.— *Epenthesis.* As examples of addition of letters to the body of a word, we are only able to present the cases, in which some euphonical letters are used to be intercalated, either between the root and the suffix, or between the personal prefix and the verb. These cases are, indeed, very numerous; but regularly depending on certain rules.

— Thus, in the verbs, which begin with one of these syllables —*ra, re, ro, ru* is intercalated the suffix *guè*, between the personal *prefix* (*) and the verb in the third person sing. of the *Present Indicative*; ex: *xa rasó,* I carry ; *re-rasó,* thou carriest ; *o–guè-rasó,* he carries ; etc.

— In many other instances it is found, that a word ending in a vowel and followed by another, beginning, likewise, with some vowel, one euphonical letter is also intercalated, most commonly an *r* ; ex. : — *sé,* my, — *ôka,* house ; — *se-(r)oka,* my house ; *ne,* thy, — *okér,* to sleep, *ne (r)oker,* thy sleeping, etc.

26.— *Epithesis.* It can be affirmed, that the addition of letters at the end of words are, either modifying elements, as suffixes and prepositions, or some distinct words by *juxta-position.*

(*) Soo in the n. **85** what moans *personal prefix.*

CHAPTER III

PARTS OF SPEECH

27.— In order to give a more complete information about the grammatical forms and processes of the Brasilian language, we will treat of each class of words, separately.

According to their distinct functions in a sentence, the words of this language may be arranged under the following headings:

(1) Noun.
(2) Adjective.
(3) Pronoun.
(4) Verb.
(5) Preposition (rather,—*Postposition*).
(6) Adverb.
(7) Conjunction.
(8) Interjection.
— All of them are indeclinable.
There is no article, definite or indefinite.

ACCIDENCE OR THE FORMS OF WORDS

28. — The changes, which words undergo to mark *case, gender, number, comparison, tense, person,* etc. are called *inflections*.

The inflection of nouns, adjectives and pronouns is called — *declension;* when applied to verbs, it is called—*conjugation*.

In the inflectional languages, as Sanskrit, Greek, Latin, etc, the various relations, which a word may express in a sentence, are indicated through different changes in the ending-syllable of the word.

Thus, in order to declare the various relations, in which the word—*God*—may appear in a sentence, as : —

— *God* is love ;
— *God's* love or love *of God;*
— love *to* God ;
— *oh!* God;
— to love *God;*
— love comes *from* God, etc ; — in such a language as Latin, for instance, all of them could be plainly expressed in this way :

— *Deus* (nominative.)
— *Dei* (genitive.)
— *Deo* (dative.)
— *Deum* (accusative.)
— *Deus* (vocative.)
— *Deo* (ablative.)

If, instead of these logical relations, we had to express the gender, the number and the comparison (degree of quality) of a noun, it would be, likewise, sufficient to change only the nominal *inflection*, as, for ex:

— *Deus*, God,— *Dei*, Gods;
— *Vir*, a man,— *Viri*, men;
— and so also:—
Deus, God, — *Dea*, Goddess;
Æquus, horse, — *Æqua*, mare; etc.

29.— In the modern European languages, as German, English, Italian, French, Spanish and Portuguese, although of the same stock, as the Greek and Latin, but not so thoroughly *synthetical* themselves, and which are, therefore, called —*analytical languages,* the various ideal relations of nouns in a sentence are expressed by the use of prepositions, whilst the other relations of gender and number, etc, continue, in a great many instances, to be destinguished likewise, by nominal inflections; ex:

— It. sing. *amico,* friend, — plur. *amici,* friends; — sing. *figlia,* daugther,—plur. *figlie,* daugthers; cf :

— Fr. sing. *ami,*—plur. *amis;*
— Sp. & Port. sing. *amigo,* —plur. *amigos;*
— Fr. sing. *fille,*—plur. *filles ;*
— Sp. sing. *hija,*—plur. *hijas ;*
— Port. sing. *filha,*—plur. *filhas.*

— « The letter—*s*—, which we find in English, French, etc., replaces the inflection of the *original cases.*

— *Gender* is equally indicated, in many instances, by regular inflections, which distinguish the *masc.* & *fem; ex* :

— Ger. *Gott,* masc. (God) ; *Göttin,* fem. (Goddess) ;
— It. *amico,* masc., *amica,* fem.; cf :
— Fr. *ami,* masc., *amie,* fem.;
— Sp. & Port. *amigo,* masc., *amiga,* fem. etc.

[The Italian words *"given as examples"* have the same meaning, as those taken from the other languages ; and so, it is unnecessary to repeat the corresponding translation in English to each example.]

Gender, number and case of nouns

30.— Such changes at the end of nouns, as the aforesaid of the Indo-European languages, are entirely unknown in Brasilian languages, the morphology of which is governed by quite different principles.

Nouns are always invariable; and, therefore, number, gender and case can be only expressed by adding some especial words, called—*formative elements* or *suffixes*.

31. *Gender.* — In the Brasilian speech the distinction of gender is only applied to living objects; and can be marked in two regular ways: either by different words, designating each one sex, or by the use of *postpositive* words, which mean essentially the *male* and the *female*.

(¹) — *By distinct words,* for each sex; ex:

Apegáua, man, *kunhã,* woman;

Mû, brother, *rendéra,* sister;

Túba, father, *siy,* mother; etc., etc.

(²) *By postpositive words;* ex:

Iaúara-apegáua, the dog; *Iaúara kunhã,* the bitch;

Tapir-apegaua, the ox; *Tapir-kunhã,* the cow; etc., etc.

32.—The latter way of marking the *gender* is also used in the modern European languages, when the names of animals are *epicene*, as for ex:

— It. *aquila maschio*, a male eagle, —*aquila femmina*, a female eagle;

and likewise : —

Port. *aguia macho, aguia femea,* etc, etc.

In English the process of agglutination in this respect is kept in its original form ; ex:

— *He-goat* and *she-goat; man-servant* and *woman* or *maid-servant,* etc.

The only difference of the English form consists in placing the *demonstrative* of gender before noun, and not after, as in the Brasilian language.

33.— *Number*. Nouns may be applied to one or more objects, and this constitutes the *singular* and the *plural*.

In the Brasilian language the plural is expressed by the use of a postpositive particle — *étá,* which means in itself a collection or multitude of things ; ex :

Oka, a house, *oka-éta,* houses ;

Anâma, a relative or friend, *anâma-étá,* some relatives or friends ;

Apegáua, a man, *apegaua-étá,* men.

« It must be added, that the suffix *étà* is undoubtedly the same word *sétà* (by aphœresis) which means *multitude*, or great *quantity*, as a noun, and *many* or *several*, as an adjective. »

34. — *Cases*. The noun being always invariable, as we said before, in the Brasilian language, there cannot be of course such inflections, as the *cases*, to express the various ideal relations of the words in a sentence.

These relations are only expressed by means of prepositions, which are always placed after noun, and, therefore, might rather be called *postpositions*.

From this general rule we must except the possessive case (genitive), which is expressed, as in *English*, by placing the name of the possessor before that of the object possessed.

In the following table we give a complete illustration of cases :

	LATIN	ENGLISH	BRAS.
Nom.	*Deus*	God	=*Tupà*
Gen.	Amor *Dei*	God's love or love of God	=*Tupà-saisû*
Dat.	*Deo*	to God	=*Tupà supé*
Ac.	*Deum*	God	=*Tupà*
Abl.	*Deo*	from God	=*Tupà sui*

« The especial relation, which is expressed in Latin by the so-called, *ablativus de materia*, is equally expressed in the Brasilian language by the same process, as the possession; ex:
Oka, house, *itá*, stone,—*itá-oka*, a house made out of stone, or a stone-house. »

Diminutive and augmentative

35.—In the Brasilian speech, no *diminutive* nouns, properly so-called, are found, as *eaglet, gosling,* etc; they are, however, expressed, either by means of suffixes, or by regular adjectives, placed after the noun modified.

The only suffix, which denotes *diminution* is — $\tilde{y}$ or $\tilde{i}$, and the adjective, used with the same signification, is —*mirĩ*, small ; ex:
Pirá, fish,—*pirá$\tilde{y}$*, or *pirá-mirĩ*, a small fish; *Putyra*, flower,—*putyra-mirĩ*, a small flower.

« The suffix *i* or $\tilde{y}$ seems to be a contracted form of the same adjective *mirĩ*: [See Aphœresis, **21**.]

36.— The *augmentative* is, likewise, formed by an especial adjective, placed after the noun. This adjective is *turusú*, great, large or broad, which, according to euphonical principles, takes the forms — *asù, osù, uasù, goasù;* ex :

Pirá, fish, — *pirá-uasú,* a big fish ;

Pará, the sea, — *pará-goasú,* the Ocean, that is, a broad sea.

DERIVATION AND FORMATION OF NOUNS OR ADJECTIVES

37.— « The primary elements and significant parts of words are called *roots*. *A root or radical* is that part of a word, which cannot be reduced to a simpler or more original form. According to their origin, roots are, either *predicative or demonstrative.* ([1]) »

These terms correspond to the expressions— *verbal* and *pronominal roots,* used by the learned linguist, F. Bopp. ([2])

The root may be modified by *endings,* called *suffixes,* which form *derivatives,* as, rich-*ly* ; by particles, placed before the root, called *prefixes,*

([1]) Dr. Morris, *English Gram.*
([2]) Bopp. *Gram. Comparée des laug. Indo-Europeennes v. 1.*

as, *for*-bid, *un*-true; two words may be placed together to form *compound-words,* as, *black-bird.* (³)

All these processes, in the formation of words, we find operating in the Brasilian language.

Although we are not quite able to distinguish and explain the roots of many words of this speech; yet, we hope to present numerous examples, which shall illustrate the subject-matter.

Noun-suffixes

38.—*Aba* or *àua* (usually with a *s*, as, *sàba, sàua*) means the place, or the mode, and, sometimes, the time and the instrument of an action; ex:—

« *Moseróka,* to baptize,— *moseroka-sàua,* the occasion, or the place of the baptism (baptistery);

« *Katù,* good,—*katùsàba,* goodness;

« *Môeté,* to respect or to venerate,— *moetésàba,* respect or veneration;

« *Petybon,* to help,—*petybon-sàba,* help, or assistance, etc.

(³) Dr. Morris, *cit.*

39. — *Ara* or *uad* (sometimes, also, preceded by an *s*,) joined to verbal root, means the actual agent or subject of an action; it corresponds to the Latin participles in *ans* and *ens*, as, *amans*, *regens*; ex:

Moseroka-sára, or *moseroka-uad*, the person who baptizes.

At othertimes, it means the action itself, as the English *Present Participle*, as, for instance,— *the thinking* persons, (=who think) and also the act of *thinking*; ex:

Morypára (*moryb* = *toryb*, to caress), a loving man, or the act of loving itself.

40. — *Bora* or *pora* (b = p) means: (1) a person who lives or exists habitually in a place, or doing the same thing or office; (2) an object naturally contained in, or depending on another; ex:

(1) *Kaá*, wood, —*kaapóra*, who lives always in the wood;

» *Mbasÿ*, sickness,—*mbasÿ-bóra*, a diseased man;

» *Mondá*, to steal,—*mondápóra*, a robber;

(2) *Mondé*, prison,— *modé-póra*, a prisoner;

» *Namī*, ears,—*namī-póra*, ear-ring.

» *Pÿ*, foot,—*pÿ-póra*, a foot-step.

41.— *Râma* or *arama* (joined to the *radical* of a transitive verb) forms verbal adjectives, which correspond to the Latin participles in—*rus*, — as, *amaturus* ; ex :

Saisú, to love, — *saisûráma*, about to love.

If the root is of an intransitive verb, the verbal adjectives correspond to the Latin participles in *dus*, as, *amandus* ; ex :

Yopuéka, to revenge oneself, — *Yopuékaráma*, about to be revenged. — « *Rama* is a postposition = to or for. »

42. — *Yma*, joined to any predicative root, noun or adjective, expresses the want or lack of the object contained in the word ; ex :—

Sesá, eye, — *sesá-yma*, blind ;

Katú, good, — *katu-yma*, bad, that is, without goodness ;

Moserokaudra, a baptised man, — *moserokaudra-yma*, a man not baptised ;

Akanga, the head, — *akanga-yma*, decapitated.

43. — *Oéra* (often with some euphonical letter, before) joined to verbal roots, means a past agent, — the person who has exercized an action in a past time; ex :

Kapik, to comb, — *kapikóéra*, the person who has combed.

The same suffix, joined to noun, modifies it in two particular ways; either converting the noun into an adjective, or making it express a thing, which *existed* once in a different mode or in better condition; ex :

(1) *Soérum*, jealousy or distrust, — *soerum-oéra*, a jealous or distrustful man;

(2) *Akanga*, the head, — *akang-oéra*, the skull of a dead man;

« *Pi*, the skin of a living animal, — *piré-ra*, the skin, which has taken from a killed animal.

« *Taba*, a village, — *tapéra* (p = b) a ruined and abandoned village.

44. — *Odra or udra*, (joined to the original form of a verb) forms the Past Participle; it corresponds to the English —*(e)d;* ex : *moseroka-odra*, the baptised person; — *iuká*, to kill, *iuká-udra* the killed man; etc.

> [The letters within ( ) in a word are mere euphonical sounds, which are very frequently used in the processes of derivation and word-formation of Brasilian languages.]

45. — We have just indicated the suffixes, most commonly used in the *Tupy* dialect, almost all of which are still in use, now-adays.

In old language, « *Tupy — Guarany*, » we find many other *formative words*, the most of which, either were totally antiquated, or are now very rarely employed.

For the better understanding of some *derivative* or *compound-words,* we will present several instances of those other suffixes:

— *Abà,* means « creature », an human being.

— *Baé* or *mbaé,* — means « thing » = the Latin *res*. When joined to verbal roots, it forms the *Present Participle*. Besides, this *baé* is the same *demonstrative* root — *aé,* which serves, now, as the pronoun of the third person singular.

— *Pyra,* joined to the *radical* of verbs, has the same meaning, as the suffix *udra,* we have spoken of before, [no. 44].

AGGLUTINATION OF WORDS

46. — Rad. *Aé* (a demonstrative) he, she, it, they, this, these, that, those, etc.

Aébaé ((b)aé, the same), himself, herself, themselves, etc.

> « The savage repeats the word to give greater energy to *its* meaning or his affirmation. »

Aè-sui (sui, prep.), — from there, from that place.

*Aèketŷ (ketŷ=*to),— to that place.

*Aèramê (ramê=*when),— then, at that time.

Aêresé (resé = from or for), — for this, or therefrom.

Aèrirê (rirê = after), — after that or thereafter.

*Aerirê-mirĩ (mirĩ=*small, little),—soon after.

27.— Rad. *Ar,* to be born, to occur, to happen, to appear, or to fall, etc.

Ara, — time, day, hour, occasion, and also—the *World.*

Araaÿbaetê (ayba = bad, + *etê,* much), — storm. « This word *ayba* is pronounced sometimes, as—*aŭba* and *aÿua*. »

Arakatú (katú = good), — opportunity.

Arakuá (kuà = the waist), — at noon.

*Arôsú (ôsú=*great, much),—to fall or to grow plentifully.

Ara-(r)*angaba,*—watch or clock; (*ang,* spirit or life, + *aba,* thing ; = *a thing possessing the life of time).*

— *Ar,* used as suffix:— to take or the act of taking.

Ara (ara=iára), —the agent, one who does an action in the present time.

Iára,—the owner, the actual possessor of some thing.

Ibytuar (ibytŭ, wind)—to fall the wind.

Ayurár (ayŭr, the neck), — to take by the neck.

Mar-ãar, (marã=mbãasỹ, a pain or ache),— to fall sick or to catch sickness.

Pôár (pô, a hand),—to take or to catch by the hands.

Pŭar (pŭ or *pỹ,* the foot),—to catch by the feet.

Pitūar, (pitū=pitūna, night),—to grow dark or night.

Tékóar (tekó,—custom or manner),—to imitate or to take the manners of another.

Teõar, (teõ, death or the act of fainting),— to die, or rather, to decay, to fail.

Tapeyára (ta = taba, the town + *pêyara,* the pratical man) , — who knows the way to the town, the head, the chief or guide.

48.—Rad. *Ibỹ=ipỹ,*—the land (earth), origin, beginning, etc.

Ibỹkoára (koára, a hole),—ditch, grave, etc.

Ibỹ-ketỹ (ketỹ = toward), — downward.

Ibỹoka (oka, house), — a wall, a thing made out of land.

Ibỹpéba (péba, long or flat),— a tract of low lands.

Ibyreté (the *r is* a euphonical letter, + *été*, much), — main-land.

Ibypé (*pé* = in, prep.), — down, on the soil, the ground.

Ibyriri (riri, — to shake), — an earthquake.

Ibytyra (atyra, a heap), — a hill or mount.

Ipysuigodra (sui, prep. = from, + *godra* = *ara*, by Prothesis, an agent), — original, native or primitive.

49. — Rad. *Ibák,* (also written *Iuák*), — heaven, the firmament, the atmosphere.

Ibaketinga, (tinga, white), — clouds, snow.

Ibakepora (pora, somebody), — who lives in heaven.

Ibákepé-o-só (pé = to, prep. + *o-só* = he goes), — salvation, — *i e:* who goes to heaven.

Ibakepétoryba (toryba, merry), — the celestial glory, *i e:* — merry in heaven.

50. — Rad. *Ig,* (also written — *Iy*), water.

Igába (ába, suffix), — lime, a thing within the water.

Igára (ára, suffix), — a canoe.

Igapó (apó, spread), — marshy.

Iggatú (gatú=katú, good), — fresh water.

Igsererusába (sererú = *sarerú,* to flow, to slip,+*saba,* suffix), — a channel

Igkoára (koára, a hole),—a fountain.

Igyusei (yusei, wanting),—thirsty.

Igotū (tū, — onomatopaic, = imitating the noise of the fall of water),—an waterfall.

Igtykir (tykir, onomatopaic,=the *drip-drip* of falling water),—a drop.

51.— Rad. *Pé,* way, track, path, etc.

*Pekoameéng (koameéng,*to show or declare), —to guide.

Peydra, (*(y) dra=ára,* suff.),—a pratical man, a guide.

Péosú (osú, great, large),—a road.

Pékú,— long.

Pérupy (rupy, prep. = through), — by the way.

52.— Rad. *Pô,* the hand, a finger, etc.

Pôakanga (akanga, the head, or the end of the hand),—the fingers.

Pôakanga-osú (see—*osú*),—the thumb.

Pôdi, — to beckon.

Pôapem, — the nail "of a finger or toe".

Pôdpar (ápar, crooked, tortuous),—crippled or lame.

Pôapyka,— the fist.

Pôpytèra, (pytéra, middle, the central portion of a thing),— the palm.

*Pôók (ok=*to take),— to pick up the fruit.

53.— Rad. *pўa,* the heart.

Pўakatú (katu, good),—of good manners, peaceful.

Pўakatu-rupy (rupy, prep.= by),—obliging man, or affability.

Pўakatusaba,— frankness, kindness.

Pўaosú, (osú = great),—courage, audacity.

Pўa-yba, — *(yba = aŭba,* bad, cruel),—bad affliction or rage.

*Pўŭbarupy, (rupy=*by or for),—furiously.

54. — Rad. *Sóba = róba,* — the human face.

Sóba(a)*pyra (pyra = atyra,* a heap),— the front.

Sóbasў (sy =asў, to be in pain),—spleenfull, or sorrowful.

Sóbaŭba (ŭb= aŭba, bad), — pale.

Sóbaosú (osú, great),—frown, or ugly countenance.

Sóbapetéka (petéka, a blow),— a slap.

Sóbapokéka (pokeka,— to wrap),— to muffle oneself up.

55.— Rad. *Tekó,* mode, rule, custom, state, or condition, etc.

Tekó-asy—*(asў,* which causes pain),—rigour.

Tekóaўba (aўba, bad, cruel, etc.),—torment, prison, peril, etc.

Tekóayba-goara (goara = ara, agent), — the guilty.

Tekòayba-moapir (mo = to make or cause, *+pyr= pyre,* more),—to aggravate the guilt.

Tekóayba-pòra—(see *póra),*—the condemned to punishment.

Tekòkatú (= *good state),*—peace.

Tekòmônhã (mônhã, to make), to constitute, to state.

Tekópòranga (poranga, beautiful), —good fortune or success.

Tekòpoxí (poxi, bad),—vice.

Longer -agglutinative words

56.— Rad. *Abá,* creature, human being.

Abá-angaypába-osù-eté,—an tyrant, a cruel man. *(Abá,* — creature, + *ang,* the soul or the spirit of man, *+ayp=ayba,* bad, evil, *+ba =dba,* —suffix— meaning thing, *+osù,* great, + *eté,* —very or very much; — literally, = a man of too great bad soul.

Abákuduayma, — a foolish or silly man.

(*Abá,*—creature,+ *kuduba,*— learning, +*yma*, without; — lit. =a man without learning.

Abámenda-sárayma,—a bachelor, unmarried. (*Aba* — (as before) + *menda* = *mendára*, to marry, + *sara* = *ára*, an agent, + *yma*, not, without; —lit.=a man married not.

Abáóba-monhangára,—a tailor. (= *Aba* (as before) + *oba*, clothing, + *monhã*, — to make, + *ára*, an agent; lit.=a man who makes clothing.

Abápórobebya(r)yma, — a proud or an arrogant man. (— *Abá* (as before) + *poro*, somebody, a person, + *be* = *ŗê*, (prep.) to, +*bÿa* = *pÿa*, heart, + *ÿma*, without; lit.=a man without heart to anybody.

Abápóroiukására,— an assassin or murderer. *(Abá* — (as before) + *póro* (idem) + *iuká*, to kill,+ *(s)ára*, an agent;—lit.=a man who kills some body.

Abá-Tupã-moetésára, — a religious man. *(Abá* (as before) + *Tupã*, God, + *moeté*, to venerate, + *(s)ara* (as before); lit. = a man who venerates God. And again: *Abá-Tupã-moétésara - yma*, — an unbelieving, an atheist.

Abaÿbaosú, a destoyer. *(Abá* (as before)+*ÿba* = *aÿba*, evil,+ *osú*, great; lit.=a great maker of evils.

57. — Rad. *Itá,* stone, iron or metal, in general.

Itápômondé (pô, hands, + *mondé,* prison),— manacles.

Itá(r)eté (eté, very or excellent), — steel.

Itá-Tupã-sui (Tupã sui, from God), — an aerolite, — a stone which has fallen from God.

Itábabóka (babóka,—onomatopaic word), — millstone.

Itábebúi (bebúi, light, puffy) — the pumice stone.

Itákantim (kantim, a peak, or sharp-pointed), — boar-spear, pike.

Itá(g)oasú (see *oasú),*—a rock.

Ita-yúa (yello r metal), — money.

Itá-yúa-yára or *Itáyubayára,* (*) *(yára,* the owner),— a rich man.

Itáyúbarerú (rerú, a vessel), — treasury, a coffer.

Itá-nimbó (nimbo = inimõ, a thread), — brass-wire.

Itápéba (peba, flat),—a plate of metal.

Itápekú (pekú, long) a lever, an iron-bar.

Itápuã (puã, standing up or erect), —a nail.

(*) In very numerons instances the *b* is found instead of *u,* and erciprocally.

58.— Raḋ. *Mŭra*, — wood, or tree.

Mŭradka (dka, a point or peak), — a branch.

Mŭra-bóka,— spinning wheel, made out of wood.

Mŭrakambẏ (kambẏ = *akámbẏ*, the groin, *i e:* the angular curve between the legs),—a pitch-fork.

Mŭrakorèra,— brushwood.

Mŭra-ẏ (ẏ, diminutive),— sprig, or stick.

Mŭrapéba (peba, flat),—a board.

Mŭrapekú (pekú, long),— a long wood.

Mŭra(r)akanga (akanga, the head), — the shoots.

Mŭraẏra (ẏra, honey), — bee honey, *i e:* honey of wood.

59.— *Mopya (mo,* to do or to make do, + *pya,* heart.) [53, 96]

Mopya-ayba,, — to aggravate, to offend, to make one be sorrowful.

Mopya-katú, — to console, to make one be satisfied.

Mopyá-katuaba-pupè, (pupê, prep. = in or within),— to please, to be pleased.

— *Monhã* or *monhang,* — to make, to fabricate or to create.

Monhangàba, — fabric, factory, etc.

Monhangára, — working-man, a manufacturer.

Yemonhang, — to grow, to prosper; (— *ye*, (particle). [See no. 97].

Moyêmonhang, —to ingender, to generate.

60. — Rad. *Nheē* or *nheéng*, to speak, to discuss, to talk, to converse, etc.

Nheeng-dÿba, (aÿba, bad), — to injure, to defame, or to reproach.

Nheengaÿba-eté, (eté, very, much, too), — to slander, to curse.

Nheeng-santán, (santan, — loud), — to speak loud.

Nheeng-sesê, (sesê = resê, prep., by), — to bind by word, to bespeak.

Nheeng-eté, (eté, much, excellent, etc.), — to speak with power or authority.

Nheenga, — speech.

Nheengaidra (iára, owner, an agent), — interpreter.

Nheenga-o-meeng, (omeeng, to give),— to promise, to compromise oneself.

Nheengapora-poranga (pora-poranga, nice or fine thing), — gallantery, corteous behaviour, polite address.

Nheenga-poxi (poxi, evil), — obscenty.

Nheengár (ár, to take), — to sing.

Nheenga-sára, — a singer.

Nheengaba, — a song.

61. — Rad. *Nitio, intio, ti* or *ni*, — no, not, nor.

Nitiokangaba, the immensity; (— *kang* = *akanga*, head, top, + *aba*, thing) ; = a thing without head or end.

Nitio-paya-oaé, — an orphan; (— *paya*, — a corruption of the Port. word *páe* = father, + *oaé*, he or she; = a person without father.

Nitiogoasú (goasú, great, difficult, etc.,), — easy.

Nitio(g)oatá-oaé, (*(g)oatá*, to walk or to be in motion), — immovable.

Nitio-iapysá-oaé (iapysá, to ear), — a deaf man.

Nitio-ipóroaé (ipor = *póro*, something residing within), — unoccupied, hollow.

Nitiomámè (mamè, where), — no-where.

Nitio-posanga (posanga, medicine), — irremediable.

Nitio-posÿ (posÿ, heavy), — light, slight.

Nitio-oikó-katú, — to behave badly; (—*oikó* = to be, + *katú*, good, = to be not well).

62. — *Pãna*, corruption of the Portuguese word — *panno*, cloth.

Pãna-ayba, — clout, rags.

Pãna-monhangaba, (aba, suffix, meaning the place, the instrument of the action), — weaver's-loom.

Pãna-monhangara, — a weaver, the maker of cloth.

Pãna-petéka (petéká, to beat), — a washing-woman, — who beats the cloth, in washing it.

63.— Rad. *Tupã* or *Tupãna,* God.

Tupãberába (beráb, to light), — a lightning.

Tupã-iandé-rekô-bebê-meengara, — Providence; that is, —God who gives to us the mode of living.

Tupã-nheenga (see *nheenga*), — the Gospel.

Tupã-nheenga-kotiasára (kotiasára, who discribs or paints),—an evangelist.

Tupã-nheenga-o-mosem (o-mosem, to publish), — a preacher.

Tupã-uatá (uatá, to walk), — a religious procession.

Tupã(r)óka (óka, house),—church.

Tupã-oka-mirĩ (mirĩ, small),— a niche.

Tupã-rokára (rokára or *okára,* street or a line of houses),— church-yard.

Tupã-potába (potába, a present),— alms.

Tupãratá (ratá = tatá, fire),— purgatory, place of punishment.

Tupāraÿra (raÿra=taÿra, son), a christian, a son of God.

Tupārekó (rekó = tekó, law, precept, etc.), — réligion.

Tupā-rekó-yabisaba, (yabisaba, error), — superstition.

Tupārekó-monhangára, — blessed, that is : « *Tupārekó,* religion, + *monhangara,* who exercises or makes ;=a man who practises the religion.»

Tapā-yí or *Tupā-yg (yg,* water), — holy water.

Tapanár (ar, to take),— to communicate, to receive the Sacrament.

64.— Rad. — *Tátá,* fire.

Tatá-ar, (ar, to bring forth, to take, etc.),— to set on fire, or to take fire.

Tatá-beráb,— flames.

Tatá-(g)*oasú, (oasú,* great),—a stove or bonfire.

Tatámirī, (mirī, small), — a spark of fire.

Tatápŭnha,— live coal.

Tatapŭnha-osú, — a fire-brand.

Tatárendy, (rendy, to shine),— light, illumination.

Tatátinga (tinga, white) smoke, *i é :* white fire.

Tatátinga-monhã (monhã, to make), — to smoke or to be smoking.

65. — Rad. *Yurú,* the mouth.

Yurúayba (ayba, bad), — slanderous.

Yurúkanhême (kanhême or *kanhŭmo,* to disappear), — to be silent, or to grow dumb.

Yurúiái (iái, interg. of admiration), — to wonder, to gaze.

Yurúyib (yib = moryib, to caress),—civility, courtesy.

Yurúosú (osú, great), — foulmouthed, hardmouthed (horse).

Yurúpoxi (poxi, bad), the same, as *yurúayba.*

Yururé, — to ask, to beg, to pray.

Yururé-katú (katú, good), — to intreat.

Yururésesê (sêsê = resê, by or for), — to intercede.

Yururé-ruré (frequentative,—*ruré=yururé,* to pray),— to insist, to urge.

Yururé-ruré-katú, (katú, good),—to pray humbly.

Yururé(s)aba, — a petition, deprecation.

Yururésára, — one that is always begging.

Yurúseem (seem, sweet), — civil, corteous, affable; *i, e:* sweet mouth.

ONOMATOPAIC WORDS

66.—In the Brasilian language are, certainly, numerous words created by onomatopœia; and we offer, as examples, the following:—

Akauã,—a bird, which, when singing, repeats this word.

Aé,—this or that, and there (=the voice of one, who indicates a thing).

Bébé,—to fly, (the beating of wings).

Gûéne,—to vomit (= the noise of one who vomits).

Iàu-ara,—dog, (= *iàu,* the barking, + *ara,* suffix, an agent, etc.)

Mobàbòk,—to grind, *(babòk,* the crack of the cane crushed in the sugar-mill).

Moposòk, — to shake a liquid (water) within a vessel.

Mopòk,—to break, *(pòk,*=the cracking of something, which is broken up).

Mosàk,— to to dig up, *(sàk,* the blow of a thing pulled violently).

Motàk,— to beat, (the sound of a blow).

Pixãna,—cat, (the cry of a cat.)

Pipík,—to sprinkle, (the sound of splashing water).

Tatá,—fire, (the crackling of flames).

Yurú-karú (yurú, mouth, + *karú,* the noise of mastication), — to ruminate.

CHAPTER IV

ADJECTIVES

67.—In most of the modern languages of the inflectional group, adjectives, in the same way, as nouns, have different forms of endings *(flections)*, according to the gender and number of the substantives, with which they agree in a phrase or sentence.

The Romance languages, principally, still present almost the same inflections, corresponding to the gender, as they were in Latin, from which they are derived.

Take, for instance, the following:

Latin— *bonus,* masc.; *bona,* fem.; *bonum,* neutr. (good.)

Italian— *buono*, masc.; *buona*, fem.; *(there is* no neuter gender.) (¹)

French— *bon*, masc.; *bonne*, fem.; *(there is* no neuter gender.)

Spanish— *bueno*, masc.; *buena*, fem.; *(there is* no neuter gender.)

Portuguese— *bom*, masc.; *bôa*, fem.; *(there is* no neuter gender.)

Latin— *totus*, masc.; *tota*, fem.; *totum*, neuter, (the whole).

Italian— *tutto*, masc.; *tutta*, fem.; (the neuter wanting).

French— *tout*, masc.; *toutte*, fem. (the neuter wanting).

Spanish— *todo*, masc.; *tôda*, fem. (the neuter wanting).

Portuguese— *todo*, masc.; *toda*, fem.; *tudo*, neuter.

Latin— *iste*, masc.; *a*, fem.; *ud*, neuter, (that).

Italian— *questo*, masc.; *questa*, fem.; (the neuter wanting).

French— *ce* ou *cet*, masc.; *cette* fem.; (the neuter wanting).

(¹) The neuter gender was almost quite abolished in the Romance-tongues; nevertheless we find some cases therein, as the above mentioned.

Sp.— *este,* masc.; *esta,* fem.; *esto,* neuter.
Port.— *este,* masc.; *esta,* fem.; *isto,* neuter.

We find the same equivalent forms of all Latin adjectives or pronouns of three endings, which passed into Romance tongues;— *viz* : —

« *Unus, a, um,* one.
« *Ullus, a, um,* any at all.
« *Nullus, a, um,* none at all.
« *Alter, a, um,* one of two.
« *Ille, a, ud,* that other; etc, etc.

ACCIDENCE OF BRASILIAN ADJECTIVES

68.—But in Brasilian languages the prevailing system in this respect is quite opposite. Adjectives are, without exception, invariable, like nouns.

In this point they offer a complete likeness with the adjectives of English, from which, however, they entirely differ in relation to their place in a sentence. In English the general rule is, that the adjective is placed before the noun, whilst the Brasilian tongue proceeds just in a contrary way.

In this last language the word, expressing substance, must precede the word of quality or of relation.

Thus, for instance, this phrase : — *a good friend,* in Brasilian can only be said — *anâma katú,* = friend good.

Gender and number

69.—For want of distinct forms to mark gender and number the adjective can appear in a sentence, with nouns of every gender and number ; ex :

Mu poranga, fine brother;

Rendéra poranga, fine sister;

Oka katú, a good house ; *oka-étá katú,* good houses ;

Kunhâ poxi, a bad (or ugly) woman ; *kunhâ-étá poxi,* bad women, etc.

Degrees of quality or comparison

70.— *Comparison* is called that change of form, which the adjective undergoes to denote degrees of quality or quantity.

The *comparative* is formed by placing the adverb-suffix—*pyre*, more, after the adjective, and the postposition *sui*, from, after the latter term of comparison; ex : Paul is better than Peter, = *Paul katu pyre Peter sui*,—word for word :— *Paul good more Peter from*.

As to the peculiar use of the postposition—*sui*, from, to denote the relation between the two terms of comparison, we find a very similar form in the Italian language, in which the same sentence above would be, as follows :— *Páolo è megliore del Pietro*,=Paul is better from Peter.

If the *comparative* is of *inferiority*, as *less prudent*, *less fine*, etc. it must be formed by means of the word *mirĩ*, small or little, followed by the same adverb *pyre* ; ex: You are less fine than John,=*penhẽ pẽ poranga mirĩ pyre John sui*; — literally = You, yourselves, fine little more John from.

This adjective *mirĩ* is equally employed, as an adverb, in sentences, like these : —I slept little,= *xa ker an mirĩ;* I walked little, =*xa uatá an mirĩ*, etc.

The *superlative* is, likewise, formed, by placing the particle *été*, very or much, which takes the euphonical letter *r*, if it is preceded by some vowel; ex: *poranga*, pretty, — *poranga(r)eté*, very pretty; *katú*, good,—*katu(r)eté*, very good, etc.

— It is unnecessary to observe, that these manners of forming the *comparative* and the *superlative* are, in general, used in the modern European tongues.

But the placing of the particle *(adverb of quantity)* after the adjective is an idiomatic usage, of which we will speak further on.

NUMERALS

71.—Comparing the authors, we find some discordances of opinion in relation to the *numerals*, which were used by Brasilian savages. The question is this:—up to what number could they count?...

— It appears, however, for sure, that, in general, they did not count objects, individually, above the number *five*, which was expressed, among several tribes, by the word *pó*,—a hand or the five fingers.

In the old documents, concernimg this point,

the writers affirm, that the savages used only the following numbers:

BRAS.	ENGL.
Iepé or oiypé	one
Mokoĩ or mokuen	two
Mosapŭr or mosapeire	three
Irundy or mokoĩ-mokoin (repeated)	four
Pô, xepô (properly,—my hand)	five

By repeating these numerals they could express greater quantities of objects, as, for instance: *pômokoĩ*, ten,=*two hands; xepô—xepy*, tventy, =*my hands* and *my feet*.

72.— Nevertheless we must add, that some living tribes in North-Brasil, owing, perhaps, to their commerce with white people, use, at present, the numerals of greater quantity, as we can see in the following examples:

BRAS.	ENGL.
Oaxiny	five
Mosûny	six
Seié (apparent corruption of the Portuguese—*sete*—)	seven
Oisé (apparent corruption of the Portuguese—*oito*—	eight
Oisepé (=*oisé*, eight,+*iepé*, one)	nine
Peyé	ten
Peiyéiepé	eleven

After *ten* begins the process of repetition, as in Latin; ex: twelve — *peyé-mokoĩ;* — thirteen, — *peyé-mosapŭr;* — twenty, *mokoĩ-peyé;* thirty,—*mosapŭr-peyé* ; etc, etc.

Iepé papasáua, one hundred, (properly *a great quantity) —* and again : — *mokoĩ-papasáua,* two hundreds ; — *peyé-papasáua,* one thousand, and so forth......................

ORDINALS

73. — The *ordinals* are formed out of the *cardinals,* by the suffix—*uara* [44]; ex:

BRAS.	ENGL.
Iepé(r)uára	*first*
Mokoĩuara...................	*second*
Mosapŭruára	*third*
Irundyuára	*fourth*
Oaxinyuára	*fifth*
Mosunyuára.................	*sixth*
Seyéuára	*seventh*
Oisèuára......................	*eighth*
Osepéuára....................	*ninth*
Peyeuára	*tenth*
....	And so forth.

CHAPTER V

PRONOUNS

74.— In the Brasilian language there are found the pronouns— personal, demonstrative, interrogative, relative, possessive and indefinite, perfectly distinct, both in forms and in uses; the most important peculiarities of which we are about to note.

75.—*Personal pronouns.* These have no distinction of gender.

There are three persons:— the person who speaks, called the first person;—the person spoken to, — called the second person ; — the person (or object) spoken of, called the third person.

These persons are represented by the pronouns:

BRAZILIAN	ENGLISH
Ixè or xè...............	I
Indè, inè or nè...........	Thou
Iandé or iané (=ia, I +nè thou)................	We, = I and thou
Orè..........(exclusively)	We, and not you
Peẽ or penhẽ............	You
Aêtá or aitá.............	They (*)

(*) This second form of the plural — *ore* or *oro* is a peculiarity of Brasilian languages, or rather of all American tongues; it means — *we* exclusevoly, that is, *we* without you.

These forms of the personal pronoun are kept identical, whether they be the subject or the object of a sentence. It is true, that sometimes the particle— *bo* is found, joined to the pronouns of the first or of the second persons singular, denoting the relation of the dative case;—ex: *Ixébo*, to me ; — *indébo*, to thee.

But this particle — *bo* —, we suppose, to be the same contracted preposition *pê (postposition)*, which is used to express such a relation ; cf:— *ixupê*, to him or to her, = *i*, his, her or hers, + *pê* = supé, (by Apheresis) — to; — *kòpê*, to the plantation, = *ko*, — plantation, + *pê*, to ; *tapê*, to the village,=*taba*, village, (by Syncope) + *pê*, to ; and also :— *orebé* (b=p) to us,=*ore*, we without you, and *bê*=*pê*, to ; etc.

That which remains to be observed on personal pronouns, will be treated of in a proper way, when we have to speak of verbs.

76.— *Demonstrative pronouns*. There are three demonstrative pronouns : —

Koahá, this ; = *kô*, here, + *ahá*=*uaá*, an agent,—the person here;

Nhãhã, that ; = *ni*, not,+*ahá*=*koahá*,—not this.

Nhãhã amô, that other;=*nhãhã*, that,+*amô*, —another.

These pronouns correspond exactly to the Latin pronouns—*hic, iste, ille,* or to the Portuguese — *este, esse, aquelle,* which keep their original Latin signification. They have no distinct gender, but they take the plural form by the postpositive particle — *êtá*, like nouns; ex:— *koahaêtá*, these ; *nhãhã-êtá*, those : *nhãhã-amôêtá*, those others.

When the *demonstratives* are employed, as adjectives, they do not take the suffix of the plural number; because, in this case, they are always invariable and must be placed before the substantive, with which they agree in the sentence; ex:

Koahá (r)óka, this house;—*koahá (r)oka-étá*, these houses;

Nhãhã kunhã, that woman ; — *nhãhã kunhãêtá*, these women ;

Nhahâamô kisé, that other knife ; — *nhaha amô kiseêtá*, those other knives.

77.—*Interrogative pronouns.* The interrogative pronouns of this language are :

Auá, who ?— It is only applied to person, like its correspondent in English, and is invariable in every case ;

Maá, what ? —It is also invariable, and only applied to things. — « *Maá* means, precisely, thing = Latin *res*, or Italian — *cosa*.

It is known that in Italian the word *cosa* may be used, as interrogative pronoun; ex: *cosa fate,* or *cosa dite,* = what are you doing, or what are you saying? = in Bras. — *maà-ta peêmônhã,* or *maà-ta pê nehẽẽ ?*.

The particles *tá, tahá, será* are used, as mere signs of interrogation.

78. — *Relative pronouns.* As relative pronoun is found only this word — *uaà,* who; it is invariable and serves for all genders and numbers.

Uaà is the same suffix, which means an actual agent, as the Latin *ans, ens,* or it is the subject of an action, as we may see in the instances, given before; [no. **39**].

The relative *uaà* has yet another idiomatical application: it is always placed at the end of the sentence; ex:— have you the arrow *which* my brother sent ? = *re-rekó será ŏŭoa sé mu mundú-an uaà?* — word for word,— you have the arrow my brother sent *which?*

79.—*Possessive pronouns.* These are identical with the personal pronouns, as follows:

Sé or *xé,* my and mine.
Nè or *rè,* thy and thine.
Aè or *i,* his and her (s), its.
Ianè, our and ours.

Penhẽ or peẽ, your and yours.
Aéta or aitá, their or theirs.

> « The possessive of the third person is very frequently represented by an *i*, which seems to be a contracted form of *aé* = *aì*, he, she, or his, hers, its, as was seen in the foregoing example ».

Possessive pronouns must be placed before the noun, with which they agree; but they do not undergo any particular change to correspond in gender and number. —[See no. 68]

80.—*Indefinite pronouns.* It is our opinion, that most of the suffixes, which are *agglutinated* to predicative or verbal roots, are, undoubtedly, indefinite pronouns. It is certain, that some of them have lost their original signification, but many others keep it still in a clear and independent way. Thus, for example :

Auá, used also as interrogative pronoun, means, precisely, a person or human being; *cf:*—

« *Inti-auá,* nobody; = *inti,* not,+*auá,* body;
« *Mauá,* whoever;=*maá,* aught,+*auá,* body.
« *Yepéauá,* each one,=*yepé,* one,+*auá* body.

Abá, creature. We think this word, identical with—*auá,* scarcely modified by pronunciation ; *cf:*

« *Nitio-abá*, nobody, = *nitio*, not, + *abá*, person;

« *Amôabá*, another; = *amô*, other, + *abá*, person.

—As *indefinite pronouns*, properly so-called, we now find these:

— *Amô*, other, others. From this are formed the following phrases:

« *Amô-ara-pupé*, on another occasion, = *amô*, other, + *ara*, time, + *pupe* = *ôpe*, on or at.

« *Amô-màmè*, in another place, = *amo*, + *màmè*, where.

Amôrupy, to the contrary, = *amô*, + *rupy*, to, by, (prep.)

« *Amô-ramè*, sometimes, = *amô*, + *ramé*, when, other when.

« *Amô-iby-sui*, from another land, = *amô*, + *iby*, land, + *sui*, from.

— *Yabé*, each. From this are derived or formed the following:

« *Yabe-yabé*, each one, = *yepé-yepé*, one by one;

« *Amô-yabé*, so much or so many.

— *Maá*, aught, something. From this are formed:

« *Intimaá*, naught, nothing, = *inti*, not, + *maá*, thing;

« *Yepémaá*, some-body, = *yepé*, one,+*maá* thing :

— *Mira-ỹ*, few, a few; = *mira*, people, + *ỹ* = *mirĩ*, small, little. [35]

Pabe or *opaĩ*, all, all together.

These *indefinite pronouns* are, as a rule, invariable.

CHAPTER VI

VERBS

81. — According to their meaning, the verbs of the Brasilian language may be classified, as *transitive* and *intransitive*.

By the use of some regular particles (prep. or suffix) the *transitive* may become *intransitive*, as well as, the intransitive may pass into transitive.

Transitive verbs are also used *reflexively* and *reciprocally*, by means of certain particles, joined to them.

There are found, yet, a few verbs, which may

be rightly considered, as *causative,* in view of their grammatical functions in the sentence.

— All these classes of verbs are invariable words, like the other parts of speech, that is to say: — that their radical does not undergo any change of form to express the various relations of *voice, mood, tense, number* and *person* of conjugation.

82. — *Voice.* (a) We think, we may affirm, that in this language there are wanting, not only the *passive verb,* but also the *passive voice* itself. First, the Brasilian language does not possess the especial verb, — so-called substantive, — as the Latin *esse,* to be. Sentences, such as; *Paul is good,* are expressed in Brasilian by the simple words, — *Pâul, katû,* that is, *Paul good,* or *Paul has goodness.* [104]

In order, then, to denote something, like the *passive voice,* it is, as a rule, sufficient to place certain words, which have themselves the meaning of passive participles, after the substantive or pronoun serving, as the subject; ex:

— « Paul was killed, = *Paul iukáuára,* or *Paul iuká-pyra; = iuká,* to kill, + *uára* or *pyra,* suffix denoting the object of the action, — as *killed.*

— « Thou art baptised; = *iné remoscrok-*

uára ; = *re,* personal prefix of the second person sing., + *moseróka,* to baptise, +*uára,* suffix, as the before said. [44].

83.— (e) *Reflexive or reciprocal* verbs are formel from the transitive by particles placed, as infixes, between the personal prefix and the verb. The most used of those particles are *ye, yo* (sometimes, *nhé* or *nhô*) equivalent to the Latin and Portuguese pronoun — *se* (acc.) ; ex :

« *Pê-iuká,* you kill, — *pé-yo-iuká,* you kill yourselves, one another ;

« *Moapára,* to crook,—*ye-moapára,* to bend oneself.

When the subject is a pronoun of the first or of the second person, it is usual to express the *reflexive form* by the mere repetition of the those pronouns, as in the Romance-tongues ; ex :

« Thou killest thyself, = *rè iné iuká,* or *ré yé-iuká ;* lit. — thou thee killest.

« We kill ourselves, = *ore-oro ye-iuká ;* — lit. — we us kill, etc.

84.— (i) *Transitive verbs* can, as a general rule, be formed from the intransitive by the use of the prefix *mô,* which sometimes works, as a causative, and sometimes has the particular function of converting nouns and adjectives of quality into regular verbs ; ex :

(1) « *A-in,* (or *xa-in)* I lay down,—*a-mô-in,* I place or I cause to sit down ;

« *Xa-ropare,* I lose myself,— *xa mô-ropare,* I make somebody go astray ;

« *Xa-puam,* I rise or arise,— *xa-mô-puam,* I cause something or somebody to arise ;

« *Sêm,* to go out, — *mô-sêm,* to make go out ;

« *Tiy,* to tremble, — *mô-tiÿ,* to make tremble ;

(2) « *Abaeté,* renowned, — *mô-abaeté,* to renown, or to make renowned ;

« *Abyk,* needle, — *mô-abykik,* to sew ;

« *Apára,* crooked, — *mo-apára,* to crook or to make crooked ;

« *Aÿba,* evil, — *mô-aÿb,* to offend, to injure ;

« *Péb,* flat, — *mô-péb,* to flatten.

« *Poxi,* bad, evil, — *mô-moxi* $(m = p)$, to viciate, to adulterate.

[This prefix *mô*, we suppose to be a contracted form of the verb *mônhã*, which means, exactly, to do or to make.]

From the foregoing illustrations we may judge, how frequent must be the employment of this prefix or root *mô*, which, indeed, is found in most Brasilian verbs.

PRONOMINAL SUBJECTS AND PERSONAL PREFIXES

85. — We call «*personal prefixes*» certain particles, which are invariably affixed to verbs with the same signification, as the personal suffixes of the Latin verbs.

In the following table we make a complete enumeration of such *personal prefixes,* indicating their corresponding signification in Latin:

BRAZILIAN		ENGLISH
Pers. pron.	Pers. pref.	Meaning.
Ixé or xé	*a*	= I or me.
Indé, iné or né	*ré*	= Thou, thee.
Aé	*o*	= He, she, it, or him, her.
Iandé or iané (˙)	*ia*	= We, us.
Penhũ or peẽ	*pẽ*	= You, ye,
Aêtá or aitá	*o*	= They, them.

LATIN		ENGLISH
Pers suffixes.	Cf:—	Meaning
o	amo	= I love.
s	amas	= Thou lovest.
t	amat	= He loves.
mus	amamus	= We love.
tis	amatis	= You love.
nt	amant	= They love.

[(*)] It must be repeated, that in Brazilian languages, as in most American tongues, there are two forms for the pronoun of the first person plural, the one *inclusive*, the other *exclusive*.

« The *inclusive* form is that presented above — *iandé* or *iané* (= *ia*, I + *nè*, thou, = we), the *exclusive* is — *ore* or *oro*, (we, without or minus you); ex: we (exclusive of you) kill, *oro ia-iukà*.]

— As we see, the *personal prefixes* represent the *pronominal subject* of the verb; but, while they can be used *alone* without the personal pronouns, these, on the contrary, can never appear, without them: We could say, for instance: *amamus*,= *ia-saisú*, we love,— wherein is not expressed the personal pronoun *iandé* or *iané* = we; but we cannot say : — *iandé* or *iané saisú*, without the personal prefix — *ia*.

— The leading rule, in relation to *pronominal subjects*, is this : — in the first person sing. it is always expressed, and takes the contracted form — *xa*, = *xe* + *a*. In the second and the third persons sing. they are regularly omitted, being in this case substituted by the afore-said *personal prefix*; ex: *amas*, = *re-saisú*; *amat* = *o-saisú*, thou lovest, he loves.

In the plural, the *pronominal subjects* need not be, particularly, expressed.

MOOD

86.— The most original form, in which the verb appears in the Brasiliañ speech, is one affirming the action or existence of an indefinite subject; that is to say, it has not the *Infinitive mood,* properly so-called, and always expresses the action of a subject, — "determinate or indeterminate". The word, or rather the particle, which comes joined to the verb, as its *indefinite subject,* is the prefix — o, and has a meaning, just like that of the German *man,* or the French — *on* in these phrases, — *man* spricht, *on* parle = *o-nhēē,* to speak, that is, one speaks.

Now it must be remembered, that this concrete mode of speech is, doubtless, more natural to savage people, who deal, very seldom, with abstract ideas.

In the grammars and vocabularies of their language, it is certain, that we find the verbs used, as in the *Infinitive mood;* but, when we pay better attention to the practical applications, it results, that the savages do not know the use of such a mood.

> [An example of this kind is found in Arabic, wherein the third person sing. of the *Perfect* is the simplest form of the verb; and this is also liable to change into transitive or intransitive, active or reflexive, by means of some particles, used as prefixes, as in Brasilian.] (*)

Nevertheless, as it facilitates the understanding of the examples, which illustrate the matter, we continue, likewise, to consider that *indefinite form* of Brasilian verbs, as being their *Infinitive mood*; ex : — *Saisú* or *o-saisú*, to love ; — *iuká* or *o-iuká*, to kill, etc.

From this simple form, which is always invariable, are formed — *moods, tenses* and *participles*, or *verbal adjectives*, by the regular use of some special particles, which occur, either isolated or grouped together.

TENSES

87. — The simple tenses are : — *Present, Past* (= the Latin Perfect) and *Future*.

(*) William Wright, *Arabic Gram.* (Dublin, 1859.)

Present tense

The Present is formed by adding the pronominal subjects, or the personal prefixes alone, to verbs; ex:

BRAS.	ENGLISH
Xa (=xe+a) mehên	I give.
Re-mehên	Thou givest.
Aè o-mehên	He, she or it gives.
Ianè ia-mehên	We (I and thou) give.
Ore ia-mehên	We (minus you) give.
Penhẽ pê-mehên	You give.
Aitá o-mehên	They give.

The «*Imperfect Present*» can be also formed by placing the verb *ikó*, to be [10-1] with its pers. prefixes, after the other verb, to which it serves, as an auxiliary; thus:

BRAS.	ENGLISH
Xa mehên-xa ikó	I am giving, = I give + I am.
Re-mehên-re(r)ikó	Thou art giving, = thou givest + thou art.
Aè o-mehên-o-ikó	He is giving, = he gives + he is.
Ianè ia-mehên-iaikó	We are giving, = we give + we are.
Pẽ-mehen-pẽikó	You are giving, = you give + you are.
Aita o-mehen-o-ikó	They are giving, = they give + they are.

—Another way of expressing the same thought is to add the suffix *ara (or baè = aè)* to the verbal root and to place it after the substantive or pronoun, serving, as the subject; ex:

« *Mehen-dra*. . . . . . . who gives at the present time ;
« *Paul mehen-dra*, ... Paul gives or is giving now [*no.* **39**]

Past or perfect tense

88.— If we had to translate the Latin term *amavimus*, we loved, into Brazilian, it would be necessary to employ the following words, — *Iané ia-saisú-an,* or at least, — *ia-saisú-an*.

The postpositive *an* properly means the *past time*. Although it is added to verbs, as a suffix, it still keeps its independent *form and import*, as may be seen in the following instances:

LATIN	BRAS.	ENGLISH
Amavi....	*Xá-saisu-an*.....	I loved.
Amavisti..	*Indé re-saisu-an*.	Thou lovedst.
Amavit....	*Aè o-saisu-an* ...	He loved.
Amavimus	*Ianè ia-saisu-an* .	We loved.
Amavistis.	*Penhẽ pe-saisu-an*	You loved.
Amaverunt	*Aitá o-saisu-an*..	They loved.

Future

89.— Now, let us suppose, that we wish to express an action in a coming time, as the expression, — *amabimus,* we will love, which is translated into Brasilian = *Iané ia-saisú-kuri*.

The above postpositive *kuri* is used, and it means, when joined to the verb, that the action will take place in a coming time, and therefore it is the sign of the *Future* of verbs ; ex :

LATIN	BRAS.	ENGLISH
Amabo....	*Xa saisú-kuri*.....	I will love
Amabis...	*Iné re-saisú-kuri*...	Thou wilt love
Amabit...	*Aé o-saisú-kuri*.....	He will love
Amabimus	*Iané ia-saisú-kuri*..	We shall love
Amabitis..	*Penhẽ-pe-saisú-kuri*	You will love
Amabunt..	*Aitá o-saisú-kuri*..	They shall love

THE NEGATION AND INTERROGATION

90. — (1) The *negative form* of verbs is rendered by placing the particle *inti* (=*nitio*) or *intimad* (= *inti*, + *maá*, thing, = nothing) before the subject of the sentence ; ex:

« I wish, *xa pótare;* I do not wish, *inti*, or *inti-maá xa potare;* word for word : = *not* or *nothing I wish*.

— (2) The *interrogative form* of verbs is rendered by the use of one of these particles — *ta, tahá* or *será*, which may be placed, either before or after the verb ; ex :

« Have you some bread ? = *pẽ-rekó* SERÁ *meape* ?
« Who is there ? = *auá* TAHÁ *o-ikó apé* ?
[*See no.* 99, 2 i,]

ANOMALOUS VERBS

91. — We call « *anomalous* », certain Brazilian verbs, that undergo alteration in the root, which is contrary to the general system of their conjugation.

In our state of knowledge on the matter, this kind of verbs is of rare occurrence ; and to speak the truth, the only ones, the forms of which are used irregularly, are the following:

(1) — The verb *só*, to go, which in the *Impe-*

rative mood presents the anomalous forms: —
ikô-en, go thou; — *pé-ikô-en peẽ*, go you.

(II) — The verb *neheẽ* (in some grammars we find — *aẽ*), to say, or rather, just equivalent to the Latin — *aio, is,* I say yes, which changes the radical in the *Perfect* and *Future*; ex:

Perfect

BRAS.	ENGL.
Xa in-an	I said.
Re-in-an	Thou saidst.
Aè-o-in-an	He said.
Yanè ia-in-an	We said.
Peẽ pe-in-an	You said.
Aitá o-in-an	They said.

Future

Xa in-kuri	I will say.
Re-in-kuri	Thou wilt say.
Aé o-in-kuri	He shall say.
Yanc ia-in-kuri	We will say.
Penhẽ pe-in-kuri	You will say.
Aêta o-in-kuri	They will say.

[In these two tenses the verb, properly so-called, is the monosyllable — *in,* and this is the form used by the living tribes of North-Brasil].

92.— Now it is to be noted:— that in the conjugation of Brasilian verbs the following elements concur regularly : — (1) the *personal pronoun,* as the subject ; — (2) the *prefixes,* corresponding to the personal *suffixes* of the Indo-European-tongues;— (3) the verb, or rather, the *verbal* or *attributive root ;* (4) the postpositive particles *an* and *kuri,* when the action is expressed in the *Past* or in the *Future.*

93.— Besides the three principal tenses — *Present,* *Past* and *Future,* the savages yet use other secondary ones, which correspond to the various and distinct relations of time in Latin verbs. They do so, by means of some other special suffixes, *(conjunctions and adverbs),* which express *condition, mode, time,* etc ; ex:

LATIN	BRAS.	ENGLISH
Amabam.	*Xa saisù-yepê-i*	=I was loving (once).
Amavero.	*Xa saisù-mairamé*	=When I will love.
Amem.	*Xa saisù-kuŭre*	=I may love (now).
Amarem.	*Xa saisù-ramè*	=I might love.

[The various particles, or modifying elements, used to express the verbal relations, may differ in forms from those above mentioned ; but, as a rule, all of them are identical in their functions and usual applications].

94.— It is a notable idiom of the Brasilian language the use of the auxiliary verb *potare,* (to wish) which does not take any *personal prefix,* and is always placed after the principal verb in the sentence ; ex : I wish to go, $=xa\ só\ pôtáre;$ word for word : — I to go wish.

The same rule is applied to *causative verbs,* or rather, to some verbs in *causative phrases,* like these : — I bid make, $=xa\ mônhã\ kári;$ — literally: $=$ I make bid ; — you can go, or you know how to go, $=p\tilde{e}\text{-}só\ kuáu;$ — word for word : — you go can or you to go know. [106]

[The verb *kudu* means, at the same time, *to know how and to be able or can* ; in Brasilian the ideas — *knowledge* and *power* are identical ones].

Except this especial use of the verbs *potare* and of the *causatives,* the general rule for two or more verbs appearing in the sentence is, that the personal prefixes must be repeated ; that is to say, — the verbs must be used, as if they were quite independent of one another ; ex :—

« I am speaking, = *xa nehe3 xa ikó* ; *i. e:*— *I speak I am* ; [**87**].

« I have nothing to do, =*intimaá xa rekó xa mônhã arãma* ; — literally: = *nothing I have I make to*.

[For better illustration on this point, see the chapter " *Rules and Remarks* ".]

FORMATION OF VERBS

95.— As a general rule, all predicative roots may be converted into verbs, — by affixing to them the *personal prefix,* by itself, or with — the pronoun, as *subject* ; — ex : *sêm,* the act of going out or appearing, — *xa-sêm,*—I go out; — *kér*, sleep, — *o-kér,* to sleep, that is, = he sleeps ; — *tog,* the act of covering,—*re-tog,*—thou coverest, etc.

Besides this, there are certain *formative elements,* which occur, very frequently, in the formation or derivation of a great many verbs.

The *formative elements,* most ordinarily used, are the two following : —

96.— *Mô,* particle, (prefix) which works, either as a *causative verb,* or converts any *predicative roots* into transitive verbs.

It may, likewise, be joined to *intransitive verbs* to transform them into *transitive* ones. [84]

Examples :

Akù, warm ; — *mo-akù,* to warm or to make hot.

Asùk, the act of taking a bath ; — *mo-asùk,* to bathe somebody.

Asÿ, pain, or ache ; — *mo-asÿ,* to ache or to be in pain.

Aÿba, bad ; — *mo-aÿba,* to ruin, to waste, to demolish, etc.

Pê, road, way, track etc ; — *mo-pê,* to level the path or the way.

Pekù, long ;— *mo-pekù,* to lengthen.

Porânga, fine or beautiful ; — *mo-poranga,* to trim or to attire.

Sài, sour ; — *mo-sài,* to make sour, to embitter.

Seem, sweet; — *mo-seém,* to sweeten.

Saráy, jest ; — *mo-saray*, to jest.

Tapy, deep ; — *mo-tapý*, to sink.

Yaseon, to weep or to mourn ; — *mo-yaseon*, to make weep.

Ye-mombéu, to confess oneself ; — *mo-ye-mombeu*, to avow.

Ye-nong, to lie down ; — *mo-ye-nong*, to put down.

Yo-yabê, to pair, or to make oneself equal to ; — *mo-yo-yabê*, — to equal, to adjust, to compare.

Yokók, to lean upon ; — *mo-yo-kok*, to uphold.

Ye-menára, to marry ; — *mo-ye-menára*, to make marry.

97. — *Ye* or *yo* (also *nhê* or *nhó*), particle-prefixes, denoting that the *predicative root* expresses a reflexive, intransitive or reciprocal action. — [83]

Examples :

Kapik, to comb ; — *ye-kapik*, to comb oneself.

Komeeng, to indicate ; — *ye-komeeng*, to appear, to expose oneself.

Koêma, dawn or morning ; — *ye-koêma*, to dawn or to grow day.

Moasuk, to bathe somebody ; — *ye-moasuk*, to take a bath.

Mo-ayba, to ruin something;— *ye-mo-ayba,* to ruin oneself.

Mosaêm, to divulge; — *ye-mosaêm,* to be divulged.

Meeng, to give or to deliver; — *ye-meeng,* to deliver or to render oneself up.

Mo-tykan, to dry or to wipe; — *ye-mo-tykán,* to dry oneself.

Participles

The rules, by which in Brasilian the several *participles* are, in general, formed, will be found in the chapter on *nouns*. [38 *to* 44]

CHAPTER VII

POSTPOSITIONS

98.— The usual relations, expressed by prepositions, as we see in the modern European languages, are denoted in Brasilian languages by means of *postpositions*. — They are various in form and number, and correspond, in their applications and meaning, to *prepositions*, in general.

The principal *postpositions* of the Brasilian language are:

Sui — denotes separation or removal from one place to another, or derivation and motion from the *interior* of an object; it is equivalent to the Latin prepositions— *a* or *ab* and *e* or *ex*; ex: I came from the city, = *xa iùr-an mairỹ sui*; lit:— I came city from.

Opè, — *in*, (sometimes = *upon* and *within*) denotes position of an object; it corresponds to the Latin prep. *in* with ablative; ex: In the Church, = *Tupan (r)oka ôpé*; lit: — God's house in.

Supé — denotes relation to an object, that is, *limitation* or *destination*, «= *to or for*, as in the phrases— to *me* or *for you*»—; it expresses a relation equivalent to the Latin dative; ex: Give this hat to my friend, = *re-mehen iné koahá xapéua kamarara supé;* lit: give thou this hat friend to; —love to God, = *saisù Tupân supé;* lit: =love God to.

Arâma — denotes also the relation to an object, but is especially employed, when we desire to express a « destination or purpose », as will be better understood from the following

Latin example: — *Exitio est mare nautis*, (the sea is *for* a destruction *to sailors*), = *pará porarasába igatinyba arāma* ;— word for word: the sea, a torment pilots to ; — I want her for my wife, = *xa pótare aé se xemerikó arāma*; lit: I want her my wife for.

Pôpé — denotes interior position, = *within*; ex: Within thy house, = *re (r)óka pôpé* ; lit:— thy house within.

Yma signifies *without*, as the Latin *sine* ; ex: Woman without her husband, = *kunhā i mêna-yma;* word for word: = woman her husband without.

Irômo — denotes company, as the Latin *cum*, with ; ex:—With my brother, = *se mû irômo;* lit:= my brother with.

[From this *postposition irômo* is derived *irômo-àra*, fellow, companion.]

Kêtê or *kêty* — denotes motion to a place, as the Latin *ad*, to ; ex : I go to thy house,= *xa-sò ré (r)óka kêtê* ; lit: = I go thy house to.

[In phrases such as : — *eo ad te, adiit regem*, etc. the *postposition*, mostly used, is *piri* = to ; ex : Paulus adiit fratrem, = *Paulú o-sò-an i mu piri*; lit : = Paul went his brother to].

Aàrpe or *àripe* — are used with the signification of « *upon* »; ex: Upon the table, = *mŭra-peua aripe* ; lit: = table upon.

Sesê or *resê* — denotes a cause or reason, « on account of, for the sake of » ; ex : For the sake of God, = *Tupan resê* ; — on account of bad weather, = *ára ayba sesê*; lit: = weather bad because of.

Rupý — denotes cause, instrument, and in a limited sense, = « *through* either in space or in time » ; a it corresponds to the Latin *per* ; ex : He goes through the street, = *aé-o-só okára rupy* ; — in jest, = *mosaráya rupy* ; lit: he goes street through ; — jest in.

Uérpe or *uyrpe* — are used with the signification of the Latin prep. *sub*, under ; ex : Under the table, = *mŭrapéua uérpe;* lit : = table under.

Renõné or *tenondé* (r = t, n = d), = *coram* or *ante*, before ; ex : Before me, = *xe renõndé*; lit : = me before.

Rekuiára, = « instead of » ; ex : Thou art playing, instead of working, = *re-porauké re-kuiára, re-yo-mosárai re-ikó*, — word for word: = thou working instead of, thou playing thou art.

[We find yet other simple or compound-words used as postpositions; but we think, they may be considered with greater reason, as pure adverbs.]

CHAPTER VIII

ADVERBS

99. — According to their signification, adverbs may be divided into the following classes: — (1) adverbs of place; (2) adverbs of negation, affirmation and interrogation; (3) adverbs of time, "determinate or indeterminate"; (4) adverbs of manner, degree of quality, etc.

(1)

ADVERBS OF PLACE

Mamé " *ubi,* where " generally used, as interrogative ; ex : Where is your land, = *mamè-tad né* (*) *retâma* ?

« This *mamé* is a derivative from *maḋ*, thing, in its most absolute meaning, — as the Latin *res* = an object, place, occasion, action, etc. + *mé* = *pé,* in ; therefore, *mamé* = *maapé,* in a thing or place. » The following adverbs will give further illustration :—

Maḋ-sui (*maḋ* + *sui,* postp. = from), "*unde,*

(*) *Retama* or *tetama* means properly native country.

whence"; ex : Whence do you come, = *maá-sui taá re-iur* ?

Maá-kety (*maa* + *kety*, postp. = to), "*quo*, whither"; ex: Whither are you going,= *maá-kety penhẽ pe-sò* ?

Maá-rupy (= *maá* + *rupy*, postposition,= through), "*qua*, in what way"; ex : In what way does flow the river, = *maá-rupy paraná tá o-nhána* ?

Ikê, and also *kô*, "*hic*, here (by the speaker)"; ex : Here is our land, = *ikê yanè rétâma*.

« From *ikê* are derived :

« *Kisiy*,= *ikê*+ *sui*, "*hinc*, from hence (from the speaker)";

« *Ki-kitê*,= *ikê* + *kety*, "*huc*, hither, (to the speaker)".

Aápê, "*istic*, there, (by the person adressed)"; ex : He was there, = *o-ikô-an aapé*.

Mime, "*ibi*, there"; ex : See my dog there, = *mime pe-mahẽ se iau-ara*.

« From *mime* are derived :

« *Mi-xihy*, = *mime* + *sui*, "*istinc*, from thence, (from the person addressed)";

« *Mi-kitê*, = *mime* + *kitê*, "*eo*, thither".

Arpe, "above, upwards".

Uerpe, "below, down".

[These two adverbs are also used, as postpoistions, of which we treated before.]

Okár-pe, "*foris or foras*, out, without," (= *okara*, street, + *pé*, in); ex : I was out, *okár-pe xa iko-an*.

Sakakoéra, "*pone or retro*, hehind"; ex : It is behind, = *sakakoéra o-ikó*.

Ape-katu, "*longe*, far"; ex : Far from the city, = *ape-katu tauá sui* ; lit: far city from.

Poiterpe or *pyterpé*, " between, amidst ".

(2)

ADVERBS OF AFFIRMATION, NEGATION, ETC.

(a)

Affirmative or concessive particles

Hēhē, "*etiam*, yes".
Empò, "*quippe*, of course".
Hēhē-empò, "in this way perhaps".
Katu-ente, "so so, or verily".
Aè-katú, "*recte*, quite right".

(e)

Negative particles

Nitio, intio, inti, ti or *ni,* "*non,* no, not, nor".

« All these forms are found, either in the negation of verbs, or as prefixes of other words ; ex : *Nitio-abá,* nobody; *nitio-mamè,* no where;— *inti-maá,* nothing ; — *inti-ape-katu,* not far ; —*inti* or *ti xa-pôtare,* I will not; — *ni-amo-ara,* never ; (= *ni,* nor + *amô,* other + *ara,* time.)

Yma, "*minus,* without. [See the postpositions.]

(f)

Interrogative particles

One of these particles, *será, taha, ta* or *pá* must always occur in the interrogatives phrases, which is to be placed after the verb in case this be the modified word ; ex: *Iné re-rekó será meape?* = have you some bread?

In case, another be the modified word, the particle must be placed after that one and before the verb ; ex : *Maá meapé tahá re-reko?* = what bread have you ?

These particles may also be joined to a simple noun, as for ex : *maá*, thing ; and *maá tahá?* = what ?

(3)

ADVERBS OF TIME

Mair-ramé, " *quum or quando* , when. "
Ara-pôkú-sáua, " *semper*, always ". — «*Ara* time, + *poku-saua*, length ; = length of time.»
Inti-an-kuri, " never ". « *Inti*, not, + *an*, particle denoting the Past, + *kuri*, another particle denoting the Future ; = neither in the Past nor in the Future.»
Ni-amô-ara, " never ". — « *Ni*, nor, + *amô*, other, + *ara*, time ; = in no other time. »
Aramé or ramé, " *tunc*, then, " at that time. «*Ramé* is also the sign of the *Imperfect*, as in the Latin verb, *amabam, facerem*, I was loving, I was making ; = *xa saisú ramé, xa monhã ramé*.»
Kuŭr, — " *nunc*, now, on this occasion." « It is also used, as the sign of the *the Present Subjunctive*, as, for instance : — the Latin verb *amem*, that I love, = *xa saisú kuŭr*.»

Amô-ara,— " in the coming time ". « *Amô*, other, +*ara*, time.»

Ana, " now, just now " ;— and its derivative — *inti-ana*, not yet.

Ranhẽ, or *raĩ*, " still, till the present".

Oiy,— " hodie, to day".

Oiypè-ĩ,—"once."

Kuisê, — " heri, yesterday " ; — and its derivative — *amô-kuisê*, before yesterday, that is, another yesterday.

Kuri, "after, presently". « It is the sign of the Future ;— and its derivative — *kuri-mirĩ*, soon after, = a little after. »

An,—" already". « It is the sign of the Past.»

Retè-an, " too late, "— « *Rète*, much or too,+*an*.»

Riri or *rirê*, "post, postea, after, afterwards."
« *Rirê* is also used, as a *postposition*. »

(4)

ADVERBS OF MANNER, DEGREE, QUALITY, ETC.

Iauê, — " ita, so."

Tenhẽ, " item, itidem, likewise, " in the same manner.

Katu-ente,— " so so."
Etè or *retè*, " much, very much."
Pau or *pauè*, " so much, or so many."
Myŭre, " as, how much or how many".
Pyre, " *magis*, more."
Amô-yre, a little more; « *amo*,+ *pyre*, = other more.»
Xinga,— " *minus*, less, or hardly ".
Anhū, nhôn or *nhonte*, " alone, only, solely."
May, " as, so."
Teipó, " at last."

— There are yet many other words, used as adverbs, which we have not mentioned.

The place of the adverb in the sentence may be before or after the verb ; but always after the adjective or another adverb ; ex: I go to-day,= *xa-só oïy*, or *oïy xa-só* ; — very good, = *katu-retè* ; much more, = *pyr-ètè* ; etc.

CHAPTER IX

CONJUNCTIONS

100.— The particles, which may be classed, as conjunctions, are the following :
   Y, — " and "
   Ô, — " or "

Aa-resè (*aa* = *maá*, + *resê*), "*ideo, quamobrem,*" for that reason, because of, etc.

A-suỳ, "*ergo,* therefore,"—(*aê,* + *suí,* = from that).

Ni, " nor ". [n. 61]

Arery, " *autem,* however or but."

Aramé, " *enim, etenim* for, for indeed."

Yôŭr, " neither, nor."

May, — "*quare,* why, on account of "?

CHAPTER X

INTERJECTIONS

101.— The particles or words used, as interjections, are numerous; among others we will mention the following :—

(¹) Of astonishment :— *âh!*....

(²) Of inquiring :— *an?*.. = what ?

(³) Of pain: *un un!*....

(⁴) Of satisfaction and of praise: *apè!*....

(⁵) Of encouragement : *érê!*....

(⁶) Of calling : *hôhô!*....

(⁷) Of reprobation : *athié!*....

(⁸) Of profound disgust : *araán!* = oh tempora!!

(⁹) Of compassion : *tuté ! auá-teité !*
(¹⁰) Of doubt : *iá ! . . . .*
(¹¹) Of approbation : *heém !*
(¹²) Of interrogation : *será ?*
(¹³) Of sending away : *atimbóra !* = be off ! . . . .

CHAPTER XI

MISCELLANEOUS RULES AND REMARKS

102. — Nouns of the Brasilian language, as was noted before, have no inflections to mark "gender, number and case"; and therefore can appear in a sentence, as the subject or the object of verbs, without change of forms.

Syntax of the subject

(I) As a general rule, the subject " noun or pronoun " is placed before the verb. The only real exception to it, we know, is the peculiar use of the relative pronoun — *uáá* —, that occurs invariably after the verb of the dependent sentence ; ex: hast thou the arrow which my brother sent me ? = *re-rekó será aŭoa se mu mundù uad ixè arâma ?* —« word for word: = thou hast the arrow my brother *sent which* me to ? » [*n.* 78]

(II) When the subject is of the third person and the object of the verb is a pronoun of the first or second person, and the verb is of the *Imperative* or *Subjunctive mood*, the subject is regularly placed after the verb; ex: that!John kill thee,= *t-inė iukả John*; [*tinė* = *inė*, thou or thee, *by Prothesis*].

(III) When it is necessary to use greater energy in the assertion, or in the expression of feeling, they repeat the pronoun-subject and the personal prefix; ex: *Ixè xa-rekó*, I, myself, have; — *inė re-rekó*, thou, thyself, hast, etc.

(IV) In the sentences, in which verbal-phrases occur, such as: — Lat. *eo petitum* (ad petendum), = Port. *vou pedir*, I am going to ask; — Lat. *venio auditum* (ad audiendum), = Port. *venho ouvir*, I come to hear; — the repetition of the pronoun, as the subject joined to each verb, is indispensable; ex: *xa-só xa senói se mira,* = I go to call my people; — literally: I go + I call my people.

(V) The same rule applies to the auxiliary verb — *ikó*, to be, in the formation of the *Imperfect Present*, as was said before [87]; ex: I am

making,=*xa monhã xa ikó*; i. e : I make+I am;
—she is working, = *aè o-paraukê o-ikó*;—
literally: she works+she is, etc.

The syntax of the object

103.— In respect to the *object,* we find the following rules:

(i) When it is a pronoun of the first or second person, it must be placed between the subject and the verb; ex: I kill you, = *xa pẽē iukà*; —thou killest me,= *rè ixè iukà*, etc.

(ii) But when the *object* is a substantive, or pronoun of the third person, the most regular use in the speech of the living tribes is to place it after the verb; although it seems, that the general rule in past times, was to place the verb always after its object; ex: — thou hast the knife,= *rè kisé rekó*, (old order) or *re-rekó kisé* (new order); —the serpent bites him,= *bóia o-sóù aé*, (new order) — or *boia aè o-sóù*, (old order).

Sytatax of the verb

104.— In the Brasilian speech, as in many other savage languages, there is not the so-called, « *auxiliary* verb », as the Latin *esse*, to be, [82] *i. e:* — a verb, which stands, as a mere connective of assertion between a *subject* and some word discribing this *subject*, and so has no meaning of its own, except that of indicating assertion, *coupling* together two words in the relation of *subject* and *predicate*. — In this language the simple union of a *subject* to a *predicate* supplies the corresponding value of such a verb; ex: *xè katú*, means — I am good, I have goodness, or more strictly, my goodness; — *rè poránga*, means — thou art beautiful, thou hast beauty, or simply, — thy beauty.

For better illustration we present below other examples of the kind:

BRAS.	ENGL.
Sakú será inè? [90,2]	Are you warm? lit : warm you?
Ixè sakú	I am warm; *i. e:* I warm.
Ixè intimaá sakú.	I am not warm; lit :
» » »	I nothing warm.
Inè ruỳ será?	Are you cold? lit :
» » »	you cold?
Ixè inti-maá se ruỳ	I am not cold? *i. e:*
» »	I nothing+I cold
Rè sekŭiè será? ...	Art thou fearful? lit :
» » »	thou fearful?
Hēhē ixè xa sekŭiè	Yes, I am fearful? *i. e:* yes, I myself, fearful.

» The verb *ikó* which has been considered by some writers, as an equivalent to the » *auxiliary* verb *to be*, — meaning mere assertion, is not so; it signifies, on the contrary, a particular condition or situation of the *subject*, that is; it expresses a concrete mode of being and the actual relation of the *subject* with the *predicate* in a definite way.

» In English there is want of this special verb; because the verb — *to stand*, — which seems like it, keeps, in general, the same particular meaning of the Latin *stare*, to be erect.

» But in the Romance languages this verb *stare* has not kept such a limited signification, and, in general, means the existence of a subject in a certain state or condition at a certain time. From the following examples will be better understood what is its proper use and import; ex:

» It. — *stò benè*, = Sp. — *stoy bien*, = Port. — *estou bom*, = » original Latin words » — *sto bene*, which means precisely *I stand well*; whilst the actual meaning of this sentence in the above Romance languages is: — *I am well*, or rather, *I feel well now*.

» The meaning of the Brasilian verb *ikó* is entirely identical with the aforesaid *stare* of the Romance languages; and, therefore, if we had to express the foregoing sentences, — *xè katù, rè poranga,* combined with such a verb, saying, for instance, — *xà-ikó katù, re-ikó poranga,* their signification, now, would be, precisely, this :— *I am well* or *I feel well, at this moment,* and *thou lookest pretty, at this moment,* — which would be different from their previous meaning.

« In short, the verb *ikó* always implies the idea of a certain *state* at the time spoken of. »

105.— Another fact, which we consider, as deserving especial remark, is the use of adjectives agreeing with verbs in the same way, as if these were true substantives ; ex : —*pák,* to awake, —*xè pák,* my waking ; —*kèr,* to sleep,— *rè kèr,* thy sleeping ; — *so,* to go, — *i-xô,* = *i-sô,* his going, etc.

In such a usage we discover manifest relics of the preceding period of the language, when words had yet no grammatical distinction among them, that is ; when all words were the original expressions of feelings and ideas, scarcely distinguished, as *predicative* and *demonstrative* roots.

The peculiar construction of some verbs

106.—A very notable idiom of the Brasilian language is the peculiar construction of certain verbs, which appear governing another verb, as their object. Thus, for instance:—

« Lat. — *volo videre,* I wish to see, = Br. —*xa mahẽ pôtáre;* literally, = *I to see wish;* —

« Lat.— *jubetis illum occidi,* you order him to be killed, = Br.— *pé-iuká káre aẽ,* or *pẽ aẽ pé-iuká káre; lit.* = *you to kill order him, or you him to kill you order.*

« Lat.— *scimus Tupy loqui,* we can speak Tupy, = Br.— *iané ia-neheẽ kuáu Tupy* ; lit: *we speak can Tupy,* &, &.

The verbs, which usually require this especial construction of the sentence, are: *potáre,* to wish or will ; *kuáu,* to know or can ;—*maasy,* to need or to feel uneasy about ; *káre,* to make or to bid make. [94]

— The sentences formed with these verbs also constitute an exception to the general rule of pronouns, as subjects, which we have treated of already in the foregoing. [102]

To need and (to) will

107. — We cannot fail to remark the usual distinction, made by our savage people, between the two ideas, — expressed by the verbs *(to) will* and *to need*. They express them by the words « *pôtáre,* and *masỹ* » — The latter is derived from the root — *asy,* to feel pain or grief; cf : — *mô-asỹ,* to be sick or to feel hurt; — *ye-môasỹ,* to be stimulated or aggravated; — *mã-asỹ,* to grow sick ; etc.

Now, let us see the distinction: *potare* is used, when they mean to express a desire or want, the satisfaction of which depends on human power, as, for instance : I wish to go, = *xa só potare,* or I desire to eat fish, = *xa û-potáre pirá,* & &. But when, instead of a simple desire, depending on their free-will or choice, they speak of a natural necessity, as of *drinking, eating, sleeping,* etc., they never use the verb — *potáre,* — but the verb *masỹ* only, which expresses a necessity imposed on man.

Indeed, we can rightly say : — we wish to eat fish, or to eat bread, & ; but we must say, — we *need* eating, as it is a thing indispensable to life.

And it is for this reason, that sentences, such as, — *I need eating,* and *drinking,* are usually expressed in Brasilian by the verb *masy;* namely: *xa-iù masý;* — lit: — *I eating* or *drinking need.*

« As is seen from the preceding example, this verb or verbal root *masy* is liable to the same grammatical construction of the verbs — *potare, kudu,* etc. [See 106]. »

Est meum, est tuum, etc.

108.— As it is natural to their intellectual conditions, savage people, in the most ordinary way of speaking, use only concrete names. It is clear, that abstract words denote a certain degree of mental culture, to which, in general, they cannot attain by their simple way of living restricted to *eating, drinking, hunting* and the like.

Hence results, that phrases like these: Lat.— *est meum,* = Fr. — *c'est a moi,* — it is mine; and again: Lat.— *est tuum,* =Port.— *é teu,* it is thine; — can only be expressed in Br. lang. by the possessive agreeing with a noun, clearly expressed, namely: *sè maá, nè maá,* = my thing, thy thing.

« The copula *est* (= is) is omitted, because such a verb does not exist in Brasilian ». [104]

DIVISION OF TIME

109.—Brasilian savage tribes did not divide time into months and weeks; at the most, they indicated the space between the one moon and the other, by the word — *yacÿ*, which means, properly, the *moon*.

a) But, afterwards, through being catechised, or through dealing with white people, they have come to designate the days of the week with special names, as follows:

ENGLISH	BRAS.
Sunday	(¹) *Motóú* or *metuú*.
Monday	(²) *Morauke-pé*.
Tuesday	(³) *Morauke-mokoĩ*.
Wednesday	(⁴) *Morauke-mosapŭr*.
Thursday	(⁵) *Sûpapaú*.
Friday	(⁶) *Iúkuakú*.
Saturday	(⁷) *Saurú*.

(¹) *Motôú,* = *mô* (formative element of verbs), [90] + *tuú* = *potuú*, rest, repose ; = the *resting-day*.

(²) *Moraukepé,* = *morauke*, to work, + *pé* = *yepé*, one ; = the *first working day*.

(³) *Morauke-mokoĩ,* = *morauke,* + *mokoẽ,* two ; = the *second working day*.

(⁴) *Morauke-mosapŭr ,* = *morauke ,* + *mosapŭr,* three ; = the *third working-day*.

(⁵) *Sûpapáu, sû* = *sôô ,* meat, + *papáu* = *opáu,* to be finished ; = the day in which the eating of meat is finished.

(⁶) *Iúkuakú,* = *ukúakú,* to fast, *i. e:* — *iú,* to eat or the eating, + *kuakú,* to put a stop to; = a day, in which *eating is suppressed*.

(⁷) *Saurú,* = *sabarú,* is a corruption of the Portuguese word *sábbado,* Saturday.

Days and nights

b) The savages divide day and night into several portions of time, after the position of the sun in the day-time, after the course or the rising and setting of the moon or the stars, at night.

We give, in the examples below, a complete idea of this usage:

Space of time	Names
From the sun-rise to 9 o'clock............	*Kôêma* (morning).
From 9 o'clock to noon.	*Koarasy-uaté*, (sun high).
— Noon..............	*Saié*, or *iandára* (*iandara*, = *iandè*, our, + *ára*, time, = our time.)
From noon to 5 o'clock.—	*Ara*, (time).
From 5 o'clock to 7 o'clock in the evening	*Karúka*, (darkening.)
From 7 o'clock to midnight.............	*Pitûna*, (quite dark).
— Midnight.........	*Pŭsaiè*.
From midnight to 4 o'clock.............	*Pitûna pokú* (long night.)
From 4 o'clock to 6 in the morning........	*Koêma piranga* (morning red.)
From 6 o'clock to 9 o'clock............	*Koêma*.

SALUTATION OR GREETING

110.— The words used by the savages, as greeting, which may correspond to our "*good morning, good evening*" etc, are these:— *Iané koêma*, good morning, that is, literally:— *our morning*;— *Iané karúka*, good evening, *i. e*:— *our evening*;— *iané pituna*, good night,— literally:— *our night*.

— The person, the salutation is addressed to, ought to reply in each one of these cases:— *Indáué*, that is,= thine also. This word *indaué* is= *Ind(é)*, thine, + *aué* also.

COLOURS

111.— Those, which they distinguish ordinarily, are the following:—

White	*Murútinga* (in compound words— *tinga*, only.
Yellow	*Tauá*, (also *yuba*).
Black	*Pixuna* or *pitûna* (in comp. words— *ûna*, only.
Red	*Piranga*.
Azure	*Suikŭra*.
Green	*Iakŭra*.
Grey	*Tuŭra*.

REVIEW OF VARIOUS AGGLUTINATIVE FORMS

(I). — To mark number :

112

Kurumĩ, a boy	*Kurumĩ-età*, boys.
Kisé, a knife	*Kisé-éta*, knives.
Meapé, a loaf	*Meapé-éta*, loaves.
Pô, the hand	*Pô-étà*, hands.
Putýra, a flower	*Putyra-étà*, flowers.
Sesà or tesà (t=s) an̗eye	*Tesà-étà*, eyes.
Taĩna, a child	*Taĩna-éta*, children.
Kôahà, this	*Kôahà-éta*, these.
Nãhà, that	*Nahã-età*, those.
Nahã-amô, that other	*Nahã-amô-étà*, those others.
Amô, other	*Amo-éta*, others.
Sè-maà, mine	*Sè maa-età*, mine (plur).
Nè-maà, thine	*Nè-maà-étà*, thine (plur).
I-maà, his or hers	*I-maà-éta*, theirs.
Yané maà, our	*Yanè-maà-età*, ours.
Aè, he, she, it	*Aétà*, they [33].

(II). — To mark gender :

(a)

Apegáua, man... (*)	*Kunhã*, woman.
Kurumĩ, boy	*Kunhã-tên*, girl.
Mû, brother	*Rendéra*, sister.
Túba, father	*Sy*, mother.

(e)

Anâma-apegáua, a male relation	*Anama-kunhã*, a female relation.
Yauára-apegáua, dog	*Yauára-kunhã*, bitch.
Pixâna-apegáua, he-cat	*Pixâna-kunhã*, she cat.
Suasúmè apegáua, he goat	*Suasúmè-kunhã*, she goat.
Tapýra-apegáua, an ox....[31, 32]	*Tapýra-kunhã*, a cow.

(*) — This form, as we see, is not agglutinative ; the gender is rendered by distinct names.

(III).— To form augmentatives and diminutives

(a)

Apegáua, man... *Apegáua-uasú*, a tall man, (=Port.—*homenzarrão*.
Kunhã, woman.. *Kunhã-uasú*, a big woman, (=Port.—*mulherona*.
Kurumĩ, boy..... *Kurumĩ-uasú*, a big boy, (=Port.—*rapagão*.
Oka, house...... *Oka-uasú*, a large house, (=Port.—*casão*.

(e)

Apegáua, man... *Apegáua-mirĩ*, a short man, (=Port.—*homensinho*.
Kunhã, woman... *Kunhã-mirĩ*, a short woman, (=Port.—*mulhersinha*.
Kurumĩ, boy..... *Kurumĩ-mirĩ*, a little boy (=Port.—*rapazinho*.
Oka, house...... *Oka-mirĩ*, a small house.

[35, 36]

(IV).—To mark degree of quality or to express comparison

(a)

Katú, good...... *Kutu-pyre*, better.
Turusú, great, large, broad.... *Turusu-pyre*, greater, larger, broader.
Poxi, bad....... *Poxi-pyre*, worse.
Mirĩ, small or little............ *Mirĩ-pyre*, less, lesser.
Pokú, long...... *Poku-pyre*, longer.
Poranga, fine, pretty.......... *Poranga-pyre*, finer, prettier.

(e)

Katú, good...... *Katu(r)été*, very good.
Maradre, tired... *Maradre(r)été*, very tired.
Poranga, fine.... *Poranga-été*, very fine or the finest.
Turusú, great.... *Turusu-été*, very great, the greatest. [70]

(V). — To express state, condition, business or office, etc.

[37 to 65,+95 to 97]

Kauî, brandy.... *Kauî-piranga*, wine, (*piranga*, red.

Kunhã, woman... *Kunhã-koára-yma*, a virgin, (= *koára*, "foramine,+ *yma*, sine", = an intact or untouched woman, *intrega filia*.

» » ... *Kunhã-imêna-momoxikará*, an adulteress, (*imena*, married, + *momoxi*=*mopoxi*, to ruin or to viciate,+*(k)ara*, an agent, or person ; = a woman, who viciates matrimony.)

» » ... *Kunhã-óba*, a gown, (*oba*, clothes.

Meapé, bread.... *Meapé-monhangára*, a baker, (*monhang*, to make, +*ára*, an agent;=*a person, who makes bread*.

Mendara, to marry or matrimony...	*Mendasára-yma,* a bachelor; « — *mendara,* + *(s)ára,* an agent,+*yma,* without or not ;= *a man not married.*
« « «	*Mendúba,* father in-law; « *mendara,*+*uba*=*tuba,* father; *i. e: the father of matrimony.*
Mirá, people.....	*Mira-resá-pé,* publicly; « *mira,* + *resá* = *sesá,* eyes, + *pé* (prep.) in;= *in the eyes of the people.*

Mirá-reapú, an uproar, a mob; « *mirá,* + *reapú* = *teapú,* noise; = *the noise of people.*

Mira-rekó-rupý, popular, common;«*mira,*+ *rekó,* custom, + *rupy,* by (prep.); = *according to the popular custom.*

Mô = *monhã,* to make.........	*Mo-apyre-saba,* increase, augment «*mo,* + *(a)pyr* =*pyre,* more,+*(s)aba,* a suffix, like the English *ness* in the word *goodness;* = to *make something become more.*

Mokáua or *mo-kaba*, musket..
Moka-óka-mirĩ, garrison; « *mokáua,+óka*, house; +*mirĩ*, small ;=*a place, where-in there are soldiers with muskets.*

Mokáua or *mo-kaba*, musket..
Moka-óka-osú, fortress, « *moka-oka, + osu*, great; *i e: a place where-in there are a great many muskets.*

Okuáu = kuáu, to know, or to be learned........
Okuáu-yma-osú, a savage man ; « *okuaú, + yma* without, + *osu*, great; = a great ignorant man.

Oyabý = yabý, to miss, to mistake.
Oyapy-akanga-pupé, to commit a blunder; « *yapý = yabý, + akanga*, head,+*pupé*, in (prep.); =*to miss with the head.*

O-yók = yok, to separate ....
O-yóka-iakanga-suí, to dissuade; « *yok, + iakangu*

....	= *akanga,* + *sui,* from (prep.); = *to remove out of the head.*
O-*pisik,* to hold, to grasp..........	O-*pisik-tajra-rama,* to adopt; «*o-pisik,* + *tajra,* son, + *râma* or *arâma,* to or for (prep.); *i e:* to take for a son.
(*) *Paja,* priest or friar	*Paja-êtá-roka,* a convent; « *paya-étá,* (plural) friars, + *(r)oka,* house ; *i, e : a house of friars.*
» »	*Paja-nongara,* step-father; « *paja,* + *nongára,* like or alike; = *a man, like father.*
Potáre, to wish...	*Potare-uasú* or *potare-opaĩ,* ambition, covetousness ; « *potare,* + *uasú* great, or *opaĩ,* everything ; = *to covet all.*

(*) Corruption of the Port. word *pae,* father.

Taba, village or town .... *Taba-póra,* free-man, citizen ; « *póra,* person [40] ; = who lives in the town.

Taýra, son .... *Taýra-angába,* a god-son ; « *taýra,* + *ang* spirit, + *aba,* (suffix) thing ; = a son by the spirit.

Timiù, meal, repast .... *Timiù-mônhangára* , a cook ; « *timiù,* + *monhangára,* who makes.

Tinoába, the beard. *Tinoába-monhangára,* a barber.

(VI). — **To mark tenses of verbs :**

Xa monók, I cut .. *Xa monok-án,* I have cut.
Re-kuáu , thou knowest .... *Re-kuáu-án,* thou knewst.
Aē o-potáre, he desires .... *Aē o-potáre-an,* he desired.
Iandé ia-páu, we finish .... *Iandé ia-páu-an,* we finished.

Peẽ-pê-saharú, you wait .... *Peẽ pe-saharú-an*, you have waited.

Aitá o-mahẽ, they look .... *Aitá o-mahẽ-an*, they looked.

Xa monhã, I make *Xá monhã-kuri*, I will make.

Re-mo-akú, thou warmest .... *Re-mo-aku-kuri*, thou wilt warm.

Aê o-ikó iké, he is here .... *Aê o-ikó-kuri iké*, he will be here ....

Iané ia-ú, we eat or we drink.... *Iané ia-û-kuri*, we will eat or drink.

Pê-rasó, you take out .... *Pê-rasó-kuri*, you will take out.

Aêtá o-mondû, they send .... *Aêtá-o-mondú-kuri*, they will send. [87 to 89]

(VII) To express the present, past, future agent, or subject:

Monhã, to make... *Monhã-sara*, who makes, now.

Monhã, to make.. *Monhã-uára* or *monhã pyra*, that who has made.

Kanhem, to fly, to run away...... *Kanhem-bóra* or *kanhem-póra*, who runs away very often or continually, — a fugitive man.

Rasó, to take away *Raso-ráma*, about to take away.

— [For further illustration on these last words, see the nos. **41, 43, 44**]

ORIGINAL WORDS

113.— The list below contains several terms of Brasilian speech, that we suppose to be, with a few exceptions, original ones, both in form and meaning.

— [Besides, see "onomatopaic words" — no. **66**].

A

A, formerly, the pronoun of the first person sing. and now used, as the *personal prefix* of the same person. [85]

Aãn (interjection), I say not.

Ab, to open, to cut, to divide, to turn up; *cf*: — *iby-ab*, to break up the soil, (= *iby*, soil, + *ab*); — *o-ab putÿra*, the flower expands, (= *o*, pers. prefix + *ab*, + *putÿra*, flower).

Abá, creature, human being; *cf*: *abá-nẽẽ*, human speech, that is, — the speech of the natives of the country, (= *abá*, + *nẽẽ*, speech); — *abá-rekó*, the state or natural condition of man, (= *abá*, + *rekó* = *tekó*, state, condition, custom), [55]; — *abá rôô*, human flesh, (= *abá*, + *rôô* = *sôô*, flesh).

Abÿ, to miss, that is, not to hit the mark, not to reach or to attain.

Aè, he, this, that, etc. [46]

Aib or aÿba, bad, evil, also an interjection, = *unfortunate! poor-devil!*

Aka, point; — *cf*: *akuái*, pointed; — *akab*, to fight, that is, — to turn the point of lance against somebody, (= *aka*, + *ab*, to turn).

Akú, warm, to warm.

Am, to be up, to stand firm, to rise up, to be over-placed or to over-rule.

Ambŭ (on.), sonorous, sounding, to sound.

Amĭ, to squeeze, to hold fast, to clinch, etc.

Ang, spirit, life, or the origin of life; — *cf*:
— *mô-ang*, to think, (= *mô*, particle [n. 96],
+ *ang*, spirit); and again : — *mo-ang*, to engender, to give life to.

Apy̆k or *apig*, to sit down, seated, steady, to be quiet, etc.; *cf*: *iby̆-apik*, to sit down, that is, to sit upon the soil,(= *iby*, land or soil, + *apyk*).

Ar, to be born, to occur, to fall, to bring forth, etc. [47]

Asy̆, to be in pain, to ache.

Asŭ, great, large, big, tall, etc.

Atĭr, hill, heap, pile.

B

Baè = *aè*, thing, this, that, etc., etc. [45, 46]

Bag, to turn, to move the body; *cf*: *bang*, turned up.

Bêbê (on.), to fly. [66]

Bòg (on.), to cleave, to crack, to be parted by force, etc.

Bóbòg (frequentative), to shoot, to burst with great noise.

Bŭr (on.), to spout, to spurt, to spring up or to rouse, to gush out with noise.

E

Êĕ, (or *aĕ*), yes, I say yes ;—*cf: nhĕĕ,* to tell, to speak, or the speech.

Ė, (contracted form of *aė*), the third person, =another ; *cf*: *abáé,* a distinct or different person, (neither I, nor thou), (*abá,*+*é*=*aė*).

Em or *êma,* to empty, to become void.

Enói, to call, to name, to call upon.

Eõ or *tėõ,* to die, to finish, to succumb or to yield, to fail.

Éu, (on.), to belch, or belching.

G

Goêne or *guêna*(*on.*), to vomit.

Guêy or *hêy (on.),* to toast, or rather, to frolic, frolicking.

Guẽguẽ (on. frequentative), to be hoarse, or having a rough voice, — *raucus,* or *husky.*

H

Hããng, to measure, to compare, to confer.

Hesá = *sesá,* eyes.

Hiỳ, to depress, to lower.

Hò = *só,* to go, to go away.

I

Iby, land, earth, origin. [48]

Iké or iký, here, to come in.

Ir or yr, to get loose, to leave off, and also (used as *suffix*) to raise, to pick up; cf: *aká-bïr*, to raise the head; — *kaa-pïr*, to clear, to remove herbs or trees; — *supïr = tupïr*, to take up, to lift; — *tïpy-kuir*, to distil, to take out the liquid, etc.

Iar (= ar), to take away, to take by force; cf: — *iara*, the owner.

Isig, to glue, to stick, to unite, to adhere, and also to hold, to catch.

Itá, stone, metal, in general. [57]

Iy or yg, water, to flow. [50]

Compare: (*)

« *Koriaikish* (Oriental Asia)....	*i ;*
« *Semoyedish* (Siberia)	*ï, or iý ;*
« *Kamtchakish* (Oriental Asia).	*iý,* or *ya ;*
« *Mandingoish* (Central Africa)..	*yì ;*
« *Erse*	*uìsg ;*
« *Irish*	*isg ;*
« *Albanean* (South Europe).....	*ui ;*
« *Arabic* (Oriental Asia)........	*maï ;*

[L'étude comparative des langues par le Baron de Merian, Pariz 1823.]

K

Kaá, herb, wood, leaves of tree, ; *cf:* ipéka-kuánha or pekaá-guána, medicinal herb, (pé = peb, flat, low, + kaá, herb, + guána, to vomit; = an herb, which makes vomit, an *emetic agent*).

Káb, to wound, to strike, to hurt, to fight. [*See* — akáb].

Kar = kari, to order, to force to make, to constrain, etc.

Kau or *kauĩ*, wine, (haá, herb, + û, drink, potion).

Kér, to sleep, sleeping.

Kuáu, to know, to understand, etc.

Kuʔkuʔ — « *See* — guʔguē ».

Kái, to burn, to be ardent.

Kô, the plantation, (the place planted).

Kuî, far, at great distance

Kuír or *kuír-kuír* (on. frequentative), to rain, to drop, to trickle.

Kuá, the waist; *cf:* ku-ár, to tie about, to gird, to embrace, etc.

Kuk (on.), to beat, to crack.

M

Maȧ, thing.

Maē, (or *mahē*) to see, to look, (the voice of one who indicates or shows a thing.

Mbaė, — « See *baė* ».

Mâmâ=*maȧmaȧ* (frequentative), to file, to roll, to put a thing upon others, to make a bundle.

Mêmê, the same; that is, continuous, uninterrupted, as the two syllables repeated — *mê-mê*.

Mēēn or *meēng*, to give.

Mī or *mīmi*, to hide, or to abscond oneself.

Mô, to make. [96]

Mû, brother, a relation.

N

Nhēē, to speak. (See *ēē*). To *nhēē* belong the derivatives:

« *Nēē-gu̇*, to swallow the word, or to be reticent...

« *Nēēg-ûru̇ (on.)*, to mutter, to whisper;

« *Nēēgêtȧ*, to speak too long, (— *neēg*, + *étȧ*, much, many);

« *Nēē-taby*, to speak incorrectly or to speak non-sense.

O

Ob = *tob*, leaves, in general; when is used as verb, it means to spread, to stretch, and also, to cover.

Og = *ŏk*, *(on.)*, to take by force, to pull, to pluck off, and also, which is squeezed out or sprung forth from one thing squeezed.

P

Pã (on.), to sound, toned, sonorous, etc.

Paâ (on.), to entangle oneself, (the voice of one who has something in the throat), to choke, etc.

Pab or *pau*, to finish, all is finished, completed; — cf: *pabé*, all, all together, (*pab* = *páu*, + *é* = *aé*, this or that thing).

Pag or *pak*, to awake, awaked.

Pánpán (on.), to spring, to shoot out, to rebound.

Pè, way, path, track, course; and from this: *pê-ár*, to cross, to athuart a place, to hinder. [47]

Peb, flat, low.

« *Pebùr* (is a *derivative* of *peb*), to swell, swollen, = to become flat.

Petèg or *petèk* (on.), to beat, that is, the clapping of hands.

Pi, the skin.

Pig, to cease, to leave off, to give over, to stop.

Pindá or *piná*, to harpoon, or every thing which is harpooned ;— (*pindá* is, precisely, the *hook* or *fish-gig*).

Pipig (on.), to boil, to gush violenty, and also to scintillate.

«*Piròg* (it is a *derivative*), to peel or to skin, etc; (*pi*, skin,+*ròg*=*òg*, to take, to pull off).

Pitá, to stay, to rest in a place.

Piu, soft, smooth.

Pô, hand.

Pog = *pok* (on.), to break into pieces, to burst with great noise.

Puká (on.), to laugh, that is, to expand, to *open one's heart*.

Pong (on.), to sound, to beat, sounding.

Pûg (on.). to shoot out, to crack.

Pûpû or *pupur* (on.), to boil, that is, the water of the pot boiling with noise.

Pūpū or *pûpung* (on.), to wound with blows, to strike buffets.

Py, foot, base, seat, sitting, etc.

Pya, heart, and also the thorax.

R

Rá, marked, painted, with stripes.
Rab, to loosen, to unbind or unfasten.
Ry = tiy, the liquid, the humor, sweat, or the current of water, etc.
Ririȳ, (frequentative) to tremble, to shake with cold or on account of fear.
Ròb, bitter, to embitter or to be embittered.
Róg = tog, to cover, covering, etc., and also to stop.

S

Sãang, to ape, to imitate the voice of somebody.
Sa-sái (frequentative), to spread, to scatter about, etc.
Sem, to go out, to be off. — [See *Em.*]
Sesá = tesá, eyes or sight, the sense of seeing.
Sê-sem (frequentative of Sem), to shed, to be dispersed, to empty.
Sêy, to need. — [See *Asy,* 107].
Sir, sharp-pointed, keen-edged.
Sóg = sák (on.), to pluck off, to draw violently, etc.

Só, to go.

Sôô, animal, game, flesh or meat; and also, to feed or to give for food.

«*Sôù* (it is a derivative), to bite, that is, to eat meat; (*sôô*, meat, + *û*, to eat).

Sỳ or *sig*, spring, fountain, origin, mother, a well. [See *Ig*].

T

Tá, to abound, to exist in plenty, etc.

Tag=*tak (on.)* to beat, to make noise.

Tai=*sái*, acid ou sour, piquant.

Tang (it is a derivative), new, vigorous, fixed, hard; (*ta*, plentous, + *ang*, life or spirit).

Tár, to take or to catch. [47]

Tatá (on.), fire; = the noise of fire burning wood.

Tātā, (on.), strong, solid, having the sound of a well strung chord.

Tōtō (on.), to palpitate, palpitation.

Torib, merry, joyful, to rejoice, etc.

Tû or tûk (on.), to strike a blow.

Tûtù (frequentalive), to wound somebody with blows.

Tùba, father. " From this word, we think,

was derived: *Tupán*, God; *Tupa = tuba*, father +*an*, elevation, superiority, or elevated, overruling,— i. e: the *father above*:"

Têtè or *tuté*, body, the human body.
Tim, the nose.

U

U, to eat and drink.
Ub, to lie down, to rest in peace; (*ub* means, precisely, the *thigh*.)
Un, black or negro; *cf*:— *pitūna*, night.
Ungá, to hand, to touch, to handlle, etc.
Ur = tur, to come, to arrive.

X

Xáxá (on.), to tear, to cut asunder, etc.

CHAPTER XII

BRASILIAN COMPOSITIONS

114.— Under this head we arrange " the *Lord's prayer* "and a few *legends* of the Indians, written in Brasilian by Dr. Couto de Magalhães in his excellent work, *O Selvagem*, to which we are already indebted for other references made in this book.

We have endeavoured to be literal in our translation imitating, as nearly as possible, the *originals*, and the only alterations made are owing to the *orthography*, that we have, especially, adopted.

It is unnecessary to be recollected, that with such a *translation* we mean, principally, to give — " more complete instances " of the usual speech of the Brasilian tribes and thus to enable the reader to apreciate, by himself, the correct application of the rules, we have stated before.

Accordingly, we will present : *firstly*, the original Brasilian compositons,— *secondly*, the English translation,— *thirdly*, the explanation of the grammatical construction and the meaning of each term separately.

NHANÈ RÚBA

115.— (¹) *Nhanè Ruba o-ikó uaá nahã ŭuák opè;*

(²) *Nè réra o-yo-moeté (t)o-ikó;*

(³) *Re-mehẽ ianè arâma ŭuáka, mamè re-ikó;*

(⁴) *Nè remimutára (t)o-oyo-monhã ŭuá-ka-pè, ioŭr* (*) *ȳŭpe;*

(⁵) *Ré-mehẽ oiȳ ianè arãma ianè remiú ara yepè yepé sui-uàra;*

(⁶) *Re-mehẽ nè ȳron ianè angaipáua resé, may-ané ia-mehẽ kurì ianè yron aitá supè inti o-monhã-na katu uaá ianè arãma;*

(⁷) *Inti rexáre, ianè Iará, ia-monhã poxì maá-étá;*

(⁸) *Repŭsŭrú ianè‿opaĩ maá aŭa suì; Amen.*

TRANSLATION

The Lord's prayer

Our Father which art in heaven;
Hallowed be thy name;
Thy will be done in earth, as it is in heaven;
Give us this day our daily bread;
And forgive us our debts, as we forgive our debtors;
And lead us not into temptation;
But deliver us from evil; *Amen.*

(*) *Ioŭr* means either, or, and also, meither, nor. [100]

Literal EXPLANATION

(¹) *Nhanè* = *ianè*, our; *Ruba* = *tuba*, father; *o-ikó*, is; *uaá*, who [78]; *nahã*, that; *ŭuák* or *ybák*, heaven; *opè*, in.

(²) *Nè*, thy; *rèra*, name; *o*, pers. prefix, *yo*, particle [97] *moète*, to venerate; *to-ikó* = *o-ikó*, be (the *t* is used to denote the third pers. of the Imperative), that is, be hallowed.

(³) *Re-mehẽ*, give; *ianè*, us, *arâma*, to or for; *ŭuák*, heaven; *mamè*, where; *re-ikó*, Thou art;

(⁴) *Nè*, thy; *remimutara*, will; (*t* sign of the Imperative) *o* (pers. pref.), *yo-monhã*, — be done; — *ŭuaka-pè*, in heaven; *iuŭr*, as well as; *yŭpè* = *ibypè*, in earth.

(⁵) *Re-mehẽ*, give; *oiy*, today; *ianè arâma*, to us; *ianè remiù*, our bread; *ara yepe yepè suiudra*, day each one of.

(⁶) *Re-mehẽ*, give; *ne yron*, thy forgiveness; *ianè angaipáua resè*, our debts for; *maŷ-auè*, as well as; *ia-mehẽ kuri*, we will give; *ianè yron*, our forgiveness; *aita supè*, them to; *inti o-monhã*, not do; *katù*, well; *uaá*, who; *ianè arâma*, us to.

(⁷) *Inti re-xare*, not leave; *íanè Iára*, our Lord, *ia-monhã*, we to do; *poxi maa-etá*, bad actions.

(⁸) *Re-pŭsŭrú*, deliver; *ianè*, us; *opaĩ*, all; *maã*, things; *aŭa = aӱba*, evil, that is, all evil things. Amen.

« May pituna o-yo-kuáu an.... »

116. *Iupirungáua ramè, inti-maá pitūna; ara anhõ opaĩ ára opè.*

Pitūna o-kèri o-ikó iỳ rupy-pê.

Inti-maá soô-e-tá; opaĩ maá o-nheẽ.

Boia-Uasú membyra, ipahá, o-yo-menar yepé kurumĩ-uasú irûmo.

Koahá hurumi-uasú o-rekó masapŭr miasua katu-rêté.

Oiepè ára ôpè, o-senôi mosapŭr miasúa, o-nheẽ aitá supè:

« *Pekoĩ pe-uatá, se remirekó inti o-kẹri potare sè irûmo.* »

Miasúa o-só-ān.

Aramé aè o-senôi xemirekó okèri arâma aè irûmo.

Xemirekó o-suaxára : Inti rāi pitūna.

— Inti-maá pitūna ; ára anhõ.

« Se rúba o-reko pitūna.

Re-keri potare ramẻ se irûmo, re-mondú piámo aé paraná rupy.

—Aẻ o-senõĩ musapŭr miasúa;

Xemirekó o-mundú aitá i ruba óka piri o-só o-piamo arâma yepé tukuman-rainha.

Aitá o-sŭka ramẻ Boia-Uasú oka ópé, koahá o-mehē aitá supẻ tukuman-rainha, oyo-sikináu reté, o-nheē :

« Kusukúi āna ;— re-rasó tenhē ; inti pe-pirári kuri; pe-pirari ramẻ, pe-kanhŭmo-kuri !

Miasúa o-só-an ; o-senõn teapú tukuman rainha pépẻ : ten, ten, ten.... = tukúra-étá reapú, iúi-étá irûmo, o-nhēēg-ar uaá pitūna ramé.

Miasúa o-ikó ramẻ āna apekatu, oiepẻ suiuára o-nheē i irômo-uára-etá supẻ : « Maá-tá koaká teapú ?

« Ia-só ia mahē ?»

Iakumāŷua o-nheē ; « Inti-maá ;— kurumū tahá ia kanhŭmo kuri ;—pe-apukúi, ia-só āna ! »

Aitá o-só ān.

Aitá o-senón o-ikó teapú ; inti o-kudu maá nhāhā teapú uaá.

Aitá o-ikó apekatu reté āna ramẻ, aitá o-yo-mo-atiri igára-pitéra pé, opirári arâma tukuman rainha, o-mahē arâma maá o-iko i pópè;

Oiepé o-modyka tatá, — ailá o mo-yotyku iraitȳ, osikinau oikó uaá tukuman rainha; o-kênar.

Aitá o-pirári ramé, kuruty-uára pitûna-uasú ana!

Aramé iakumāyua o-nheē : « Ia-kanhŭmo! «Kunhã mokú (s)óka ôpè o-kudu-an iané ia-pirári koahá tukuman-rainha! »

Aitá o-só ān.

Kunhã moku sóka ôpè o-nheē i mêna supè : « Aitá opirari pitūna. Kuȳr ia-só ia-sarú koêma ».

Aramé opaī maá, o-sáin oikó uaa kaá rupy, oyseréo soô arâma, uyrá arâma.

Opaī maá, o-sáin oikó paraná rupy, oyerèo ipéká arâma, pirá arâma;
Uru-sakanga o-yeréo iáuára-eté arâma ; pirakasára oyseréo i igára irūmo ipeka arâma: i akanga ipék-akanga arâma ;— i igâra ipèka setè arāma ; i apukuitáua oyeréo ipèka-rétima arâma.

Boia-Uasu membyra o-mahē ramé yasi-táta-uasu, o-nheē i mēna supé: «Koēma o-iur oikó; xa só xa moīn ara pitûna sui. »

Aramè aè o-mamán inimô, o-nheē : «Indé cuyubī kuri, o-nheēgar arāma, koēma o-iur ramè kuri.» Kodi o-monhā cuyubī : o-mo-piranga i setima uruku irûmo, o-motinga i akanga tabatinga irumo ; — o-nheē ixupè : «Re-nheēgar-kuri opaī ará opè, koēma o-iur ramè !

Ariré aè o-mamán inimô, o-nheé : — «Indé inambu kuri.»

O-pisika tanimuka, omburi sesè, o-nheē i-xupè:—«Inè inambu kuri, onheēngár arama kuruka ramè, pitūna ramè, pŭsaié ramé, pitunapoku ramè, koêma piranga ramè.» [10ᵒ, b]

Aá-sui uyrá-étá o-nheēgár ára katu ôpé, koêma o-ur ramè, omorôri arama ára.

Mosapŭr miasua o-sŭka ramé, kurumī-uasu o-nheē aitá supè : «Penhē inti pe-supi-uâna ! «Penhē pe-pirári pituna; Penhē pe-monhā uān opaī maá okā-yma ! Aarsé pe-yeréo makakai arāma opaī ára opé ;— pe-uatá mŭra-rakanga rupy eatíre....

‹ HOW NIGHT BEGAN ›

In the *beginning* there was no night ; — day only was all time ;

The night was sleeping in the depth of waters ;
There were no animals ; all things spoke ;

The daughter of the *Great Serpent*, they tell, had married to a young-man;

This young-man had three faithful servants.

One day he called these three servants and said to them.

— « Go and walk, because my wife is unwilling to sleep with me; »

The servants went away; and then he called his wife to sleep with him;

The daughter of the *Great Serpent* replied to him:

"It is night not yet".

The young-man said to her: — There is no night; day only is all time;

The young-woman spoke: — « my father possesses the night.

« If you want to sleep with me, bid seek it there on the river. »

The young-man called the three servants;

The young woman ordered them to go to her father's house and to bring a stone of tucumãn; (*)

The three servants went out, arrived at the house of the *Great Serpent*; — this gave them a stone of tucumãn, completely closed, and said to

---

(*) *It is a Brasilian palm-tree.*

them : — « Here it is; take it. — Take care! Do not open it, otherwise all of you shall perish ! »

The servants returned, and were hearing noise within the stone of tucumán, thus : — *tin, tin, tin, xi... xi, xi...*, it was the note of the cricket and of the small frogs, who sing at night.

When they were far already, one of them said to his companions : — « Let us see what noise is this? »

The pilot observed: « No; else, we shall be lost. Let us go away ; — pull the oars ! »

They went on, and continued to hear that noise within the stone of tucuman, and could not understand what noise was that;

When they were far off, they assembled in the middle of the canoe, — lighted a fire, melted the pitch, which covered the stone, and opened it.

Suddenly all grew dark !

The pilot, then, said: « We are lost! The young-woman, at home, knows already, that we opened the stone of tucuman ! »

They went on their voyage.

The young-woman at home said then to her husband : —

« They delivered night; Let us wait for the morning. »

At this time all the things, which were scattered throughout the wood, became transformed into animals and birds;

The things, which were scattered throughout the river, were transformed into goose and fish.

From the basket was engendered the panther; the fisher with his canoe was transformed into a goose:— from his head sprang the head and bill of the goose; — from the canoe sprang the body of the goose; — from the oars sprang the legs of the goose.

— The daughter of the *Great Serpent*, when she saw *Venus* (star), said to her husband: « Dawn approaches; I go to separate the day from the night. »

Then she rolled up a thread, and said: « Thou shalt be a *cuyubin*. » So she made the *cuyubin*. She painted the head of the *cuyubin* white with *tabatinga* (clay); she painted his legs red with *urucù* (a red fruit), and, then, she said: « Thou shalt sing, for ever, when morning breaks. »

— She rolled up, again, the thread, scattered ashes over it, and said: « Thou shalt be *inambù*, to sing during the whole time of the night and of the dawn. »

— Thenceforward, all birds have sung at

their determined times, and all together sing at dawn to rejoice the beginning of day...

— When the three servants arrived, the young-man said to them: — « You were not faithful; you opened the stone of *tucumân;* you set free [night; all things were lost, — and you, yuorselves, who shall be transformed into *monkeys,* — and shall walk, for ever, climbing on the branches of trees!....................

Literal TRANSLATION

Iupirungáua ramè, inti-maá pitūna; ara anhõ opaĩ ára opè.
Beginning when, nothing night: day alone all time at.

Pitūna o-kéri o-ikó iy rupy-pè.
Night slept it was water's-depth within.

Inti-maá soô-étá; opaĩ maá o-nheẽ.
Nothing animals; all things spoke.

Boia-Uassú membỹra, ipahá, o-yo-menar yepè kurumi-uasú irúmo.

Serpent-Great's daughter, they tell, married one boy big with.

Koahá kurumi-uasú o-rekó mosapŭr miasúa katu-reté.

This boy big had three servants faithful very.

Oiepè ara ôpè, o-senôĩ mosapŭr miasúa, o-nheē aitá supè:

One day at, he called three servants, said them to:

« *Pēkoē, pê-uatá; se remirekó inti o-kèri potare sè irûmo.* »

« Go, walk; my wife not sleep will me with. »

Miasua o-so-an.

Servants went.

Aramè aè o-senôi xemirekó okeri arâma aè irûmo:

Then he called his wife sleeping for, him with.

Xemirekó o-suaxára: Inti raĩ pitûna.

Wife replied: Not yet night.

Inti-maá pitūna; ara anhō.

Nothing night; day alone.

Se ruba o-rekó pitûna.

My father has night.

Re-keri polare ramè se irumo, re-môndu piâmo aè paraná rupy.

Thou sleep to wantest if me with, bid seek it river on.

Aè o-senõi mosapŭr miasua;

He called three servants;

Xemirekó o-môndu aitá ì ruba oka piri, o-só opiamo arãma yepè tukuman rainka.

Wife bade them her father's house to, to go to seek for one tucuman-stone.

Aitá o-sŭka ramè, Boia-Uasu oka ôpè, koahá o-mehẽ aitá supè oiepè tukuman-rainha oyo-sykináu reté, o-nheẽ:

They arrived when, Serpent-Great's house at, this gave them to one tucuman-stone closed quite, she said:

" Kusukuí ána ; re-rasó tenhẽ ; inti pẽ-pirari-huri; pẽ-pirári ramè, pé-kanhŭmo kuri "

« Here it; take with you; not open shall; open if, you be lost shall. »

Miasúa o-só àn, o-senoñ teapú tukuman-rainha pôpè: — ten-ten, ten-ten... = tukùra-étá reapú iùì-étá irũmo, o-nheẽgar uaá pitûna ramè.

Servants went away, they heard noise tucuman-stone within:—tín-tin, ten-tem... = cricket's noise small-frogs with, sing who night when.

Miasùa o-ikó ramé âna apekatú, oiepé sui-uára o-nheẽ i irumo-uara-etá supé: " Maá tá koahá teapú? — Ia-só ia-mahẽ?

Servants were when already far off, one of them said his companions to: — " What this noise? We go we see?

Iakumãyua o-nheẽ: "Inti-maá; kurumũ tahá ia-kanhũmo kuri; — pẽ-apukúi, ia-só ana!

Pilot said: " Never; otherwise we be lost shall; pull the oars, let us go away!

Aitá o-só an.

They went away.

Aitá o-senon o-ikó teapú; inti o-kuáu maá nhahã teapú uda.

They hear they were noise, not they understood that noise what.

Aita o-ikó apekatú-reté ãn ramé, aitá o-yomoatiri igara-pitéra opé, opirári ardma maã oikó i pôpé...

They were far off when, they grouped canoe-middle in, open to tucunam-stone, see to what was its inside.

Oiepé o-modýk tatá; aitá o-moyotikũ iraitỹ, o-sikindu o-ikó uaá tukuman-rainha; — o-kẽnar.

One lighted fire; they melted the pitch, covering was which tucuman-stone; they opened...

Aitá opirări ramé, kuruty-uara pitūna-uasú ăna!

They opened when, suddenly night every where!

Aramé iakumáyua o-nheẽ: " Ia-kanhŭmo! Kunhã-mohú sóka ôpè — o-kuáu-an ianè ia-pirari ko-aká tukuman-rainha!"

Then pilot said : " We are lost! Young woman house at knew already we opened this tucuman-stone!"

Aitá o-só an...

They went on.

Kunhã-mokú soka ôpè o-nheẽ i mẽna supè: « Aitá o-pirári pitûna.

Young-woman house at, said her husband to: « They opened night.

« *Kuăr ia-só ia-sarú koêma.* »

« Now, we go we wait morning. »

Aramè opaĩ maá o-sain, o-ikó uaá kaá rupy, oyeréu soô arãma, uyrá arãma.

Then all things scattered, were which wood throughout, transformed animals into, birds into.

Opaĩ-maá o-sain, o-ikó uaá paraná rupy, oyeréu ipèka arãma, pirá arãma.

All things scattered, were which river throughout, transformed goose into, fish into.

Uru-sakanga oyeréu idudra-eté arâma; pirá-kasára oyeréu i igára iromo ipeka arâma: i akanga, ipeka akanga arâma; — i igára, ipeka-seté arama; — i apukuitáua oyeréu ipeka retima arâma.

Basket became transformed panther into; fisher was transformed his canoe with goose into: his head goose'shead into; his canoe goose's body into; his oars were transformed goose's legs into.

Boia-Uasù membyra o-mahẽ ramè yasi-tatá-uásu, o-nheẽ i mena supè: « Koéma o-iùr o-ikó; xa só xa moĩn ara pitũna sui. »

Serpent-Great's daughter saw when star-fire great, said her husband to: « Dawn comes it is, I go I divide day night from. »

Aramé ai o-maman inimõ, o-nheẽ: « Indé cuyubĩ kuri, o-nheẽg-ar arâma koéma o-ur ramè kuri. » Koai o-monhã cuyubĩ: —

Then she rolled up a thread, said: « Thou cuyubin shalt, sing to morning come when shall ». So she made cuyubin.

O-mopiranga i setima urukú irûmo, — omotinga i akanga tabatınga irumo; o-nheẽ i-xupè: —« Re-nheẽg-ar kuri opaĩ ara opé koema o-iur ramè. »

She whitened his head white clay with, she *reddened* his legs *urucú* with; she said him to:

« Thou sing shalt all time at, morning comes when.

Aramè aè o-mamán inimô, o-nheẽ: « *Indé inambú kuri.* »

After she rolled up the thread, said: « Thou inambú shalt.

O-pisíka tanimuka, ombúre sesé, o-nheẽ i-xupè: « *Iné inambú kuri, onheẽg-ar arâma, karuka ramé, pitûna ramé, pŭsaiè ramé, pitûna-pokú ramé, koema piranga ramé* [109, b].

She took ashes, scattered on it, said him to: « Thou inambú shalt, sing to, evening at, and during the whole night... [109, b].

Aà-sui uyrá-età o-nheẽgar ara katú ôpè, koêma o-iúr ramè, omororỹ arâma ára.

Thenceforward birds sing times determined at, and morning comes when, rejoice to day..

Mosapŭr miasua o-sŭka ramè, kurumĩ-uasú o-nheẽ aità supé: « *Penhẽ inti pe-supi-uân!* « *Penhẽ pe-pirári pituna. Penhẽ pe-monhã uân opaĩ-maā okayma; aarsé pe-yeréu makakái arâma opaĩára opé; pe-uatá mŭra-rekanga rupy eatire!....* »

Three servants arrived when, young-man said them to: « You not faithful were! You delivered night. You made all things be lost;

therefore you shall become monkeys into, ever for ; you shall walk tree-branches over climbed!...»

KUNHÃ-MOKU O-SÓ UAÁ O-SIKARI MENA

I

Kunhã-môkù, Mykùra

117. *Oiépè kunhã-mokù o-nhẽẽ i sy supè :*
« *Xa só xa sìkari se ména ;*
« *Xa purardre rêtè iu-masy !* »
Aè o-só ãn ; o-sŭka o-ăn, mamé o-ikó môsa-pŭr pê, o-puranú : maá-tá Inayé pé ? (*)
Oiepè pé ôpe, aè o-mahẽ inambu-ráua ; aramé aè o-maité-oãn : — Koahá Inayé pé.
O-só-ãn aè rupy.
Opausápe, o-yo-iúanti óka, mamè o-ikó yepè uáimi ó-apyk-oikó uaá tatá remehŭpe ; o-nhẽẽ :
Inè será Inayé sy ?
Uáimi o-suaxára : — Ixè aè tenhẽ.

(*) *Inayé* is the Brasilian name of a sparrow-hawk, very beautiful and rapacious. And as it seems natural, what is fine and able to get plenty of food is considered by the savage, as the richest and the best one.

Kunhã-mokù o-nhẽẽ : Xa iùr aè piri xa menar arâma aè irùmo.

Uaimi o-nhẽẽ: — se mbyra mira poxi-retè aè; aa-resê xa sò xà iumimi inè.

Kôahà uaimi inti Inayè sy; Mykùra (*) sy aè.

Karuka ramè i mbyra o-sŭka-oân; o-rure-an xemiàra, = uirà-età.

I sy o-mongaturù aità o-ù arama.

Aità o-ù o-ikò ramè, i sy o-puranù i-xuì: O-sŭka ramè oiepè amo tetama-uàra, mày tahà re-reko aè?

Mykùra o-suaxàra: Xa senòi aè o-ù arâma ianè irùmo.

Aramè uaimi o-senoi kunhã mokù, o-iumimi o-ikò uaâ.

Kunhã-moku o-ù-ãn aità irûmo.

Mykùra sorib o-ikò, maa-resè kunhã-mokù poranga rête.

Pitùna opè, mykùra o- sò ramè, okèr arâma kunhã mokù irûmo, aè ompù-ân aè o-nhẽẽ :

Inti xa ienõ potàre nè irùmo, maa-resè inêma rêtè inè.

Koêma ramè, uaimi o-mondù ramè kunhã mokù o-iuùka iepea, kunhã mokù o-iauàu-ãn.

(*) Animal like a fox.

II

Kunhã mokú, Urubú

O-sŭka mosapŭr pê ôpè, o-só amô rupy;
O-sŭka òka ôpè, o-iǔuanti amô uáimi irûmo;
O-puranû i-xui: Indè será Inayé sy?
Uáimi o-suaxára: — Ixè aè tenhē.
Kunhã mokú o-nhēē: xa ùr aè piri, xa menar arâma aè irûmo.
Uáimi onhēē: Xa só xa iumimi indè, se mbyra poxi retè sesé.
Koahá uáimi urubú sy.
Karuka ramè, i mbyra o-sŭka; o-rúrè xemiára, = itápurú miriétá, onhēhē i sy supè:
« Kusukui pirá miritá, se sy. »
I sy o-monguturú ximiára.
Aitá o-ù oikó ramè, aè o-puranú:
Auá supè o-sŭka uaá amô tetâma suí, maá-tá re-monhã i-xupé?
Urubú o-suaxára: xa senoi aè o-u arâma ianè irûmo.
Aramè i sy o-senoi kunhã-moku.
Urubú sorib-etè an, kunhã-moku poranga retè resè.

Pitûna ôpè, aè o-só ramé o-yenõ aè irumo, kunhã-mokù ompù-àn, inēma resé aè.

Amô koēma ôpè, uáimi o-mondù ramè kunhã mokù o-iuuka arama iapeá, kunhã-mokù o-iauau-ãn....

III

« Kunhã-mokú, Inayé »

Aè o-sŭka ramè mosapŭr pê ôpè, o-só amô rupy.

O-sŭka oka ôpè, o-mahē yepè udimi poranga-reté, o-puranù i-xui :— Iné Inayè sy será ?

Udimi o-suaxára : Ixè aè tenhē.

Kunhã-moku o-nhēõ : xa-ur aè piri xa menar arama aè irumo.

Uaimi o-nhēē : xa só xa-iumimi indé ; sè mbỳra mira poxî-reté !

Karuka ramè, mbyra o-sŭka ; o-rùre ximidra, = uirá-mìrĩ-tá.

I sy omon-gaturù uĭra mirĩtá aitá où arãma.

Aitá où o-ikó ramè, i sy o-puranù i-xui :

Auá supè o-sŭka uaã ramè amô tetãma sui, maã tà re-monhã i-xupè?

*Inayé o-suaxára: — Xa-senoi aè oú arãma
iané irŭmo.*

Aramè uáimi o-senoi kunhã-mokú.

*Inayè sorib reté, kunhã mokú poranga reté
resè.*

Aetá o-keri-an iepe-uasú.

*Amo ara-ôpé, Urúbú o-sŭka Inayè oka ôpé,
o-sikari arãma kunhã mokú.*

*Aitá omara-monhã-oan retè kunhã-mokú
resè.*

Inayè ompŭk-ãn Urubú akanga.

I sy omo-akú iy, mo-asúk i akanga.

*Iy sakú reté oãn; aaresé i akanga-saua-yma
opitá ara opé.* . . . .

"THE YOUNG-WOMAN WHO GOES TO SEEK HUSBAND"

I

" The Young-woman and the Fox "

One day, a young-woman said to her mother:
"I go to seek my husband; I am feeling great
hunger".

She went away; arrived wherein there were
three paths, and asked :— which is the Inaye's
path ?. . . .

In the one path, she saw some feathers of inambù; then she thought:— This must be the Inayé's path.

She went along this.

At last, she met a house, where was an old woman seated at the fire-side, and asked to her: " Are you the Inayé's mother? "

The old-woman replies : — I, myself, yes.

The young-woman said: I come to marry with him.

The old woman said:— " My son is a very *troublesome fellow*! Therefore I go to hide you."

This old woman was not the mother of Inayé, but she was the Fox's mother.

In the evening, her son came back, and brought his game,= birds.

His mother tempered them for eating; and when they were eating, the mother asked to son:— if now somebody came here from other land, how should you treat him?

The Fox replied:— I would call him to eat with us.

Then the old woman called the young-woman, who was hidden.

This ate with them.

The Fox became very content, because she was very beautiful.

At night, the Fox went to sleep with the young-woman; but this expelled him, saying, that he was too stinking.

When in the morning the old woman bade the young-woman seek fuel, this went away, and...

II

« The Young-woman and the Carrion-Crow. »

She arrived at three paths, and went through another...

At last, she arrived at a house, where she met other old woman, to whom she asked: — Are you the Inayé's mother?

The old woman replied: Yes, I am.

The young-woman said: I come to marry with him.

The old-woman said: I go to hide you, because my son is a very troublesome fellow!

This old-woman was the Carrion-crow's mother.

At evening, her son arrived; he brought small worms, and said to his mother: "Here is small fish, mother".

His mother tempered the prey.

When they were eating, she spoke: — If somebody came now from other land, how should you treat him ?

The Carrion-crow replied: I would call him to eat with us.

Then his mother called the young-woman.

The Crow became very content, because she was very fine.

At night, he went to sleep with the young-woman, but this expelled him on account of his stinking.

In the other morning, when the old-woman bade the young-woman seek fuel, she run away...

III

« The Young-woman and the Sparrow-hawk. »

She arrived, again, at three paths, and she went through another...

She arrived at a house, where she met a fine old-woman, to whom she asked: Art thou the Inayé's mother?

The old-woman replied: Yes, I am.

The young-woman said: I come to marry with him.

The old-woman said: I go to hide you, because my son is a very troublesome fellow!

At evening, the son arrived and brought his game, = many small birds.

His mother prepared the birds for their eating; and when they were eating, she asked to him: « If somebody came from other land, how should you treat him? »

Inayé replied: I would call him to eat with us. Then the old-woman called the young-woman.

Inayé became very glad, because she was very fine.

They slept together.

In the other day, the Carrion-crow arrived at Inayé's house, looking for the young-woman. They fighted much on account of the young-woman.

Inayé brake open the head of the Crow.

The mother of the latter warmed water, washed his head; but the water was too warm, and, therefore, his head became bald, since then..

Literal TRANSLATION

I

« KUNHÃ-MOKU, MYKURA »

« The Young-woman and the Fox »

Oiépè kunhã-mokú o-nhēē i sy supè: « *Xa só xa sìkari se mêna ;*

A young-woman said her mother to : « I go I seek my husband ;

« *Xa puraráre rêtè iu-masy !* »

« I feel great hunger. »

Aè o-só ān ; o-sŭka o-ăn, mamé o-ikó môsapŭr pè, o-puranù: — Maá-ta Inayé pê ? (*)

« She went away ; arrived, where there were three paths, she asked: — Which Inayé's path ?

Oiepè pé ôpe, aè o-mahē inambu-ráua ; aramé aè o-maité-oān: — Koahá Inayé pê.

One path in, she sees inambu's feathers ; then she thought : This Inayé's path.

O-só-ān aè rupy.

She went along this through.

(*) *Inayé* is the Brasilian name of a sparrow-hawk.

Opausàpe, o-yo-iùanti òka, mamé o-ikò yepè udimi ô-apik-oikò uaà tatà remehŭpe; o-nhẽẽ:

At last, she met a house, where was one old woman seated was who fire-side at; she said:

« *Inè serà Inaye sy?* »

« You Inayé's mother? »

Udimi o-suaxàra: — Ixè aè tenhẽ

The old-woman replied: — I myself yes.

Kunhã-mokù o-nhẽẽ: Xa iùr aè piri xa menar arâma aè irùmo.

The young-woman said: — I come him to, I to marry him with.

Uaimi o-nhẽẽ: — se mbyra mira poxi-reté aè; aa-rèsê xa sò xà iumimi inè.

The old woman says: my son *bad very he*; therefore I go I hide you.

Kôahà udimi inti Inaye sy; Mykùra(*) sy aè.

This old woman not Inayé's mother; Fox's mother she.

Karuka ramè, i mbyra o-sŭka-oân; o-rure-an xemiàra, — uira-età.

Evening when, her son came back; he brought his game, — birds.

(*) Animal like a fox.

I sy o-mongaturu aità o-u arama.
His mother tempered them eating for.

*Aità o-ù o-ikò ramè, i sy o-puranù i-xui:
O-sŭka ramè oiepè amô tetama-uára, máy tahà re-rekò aè?*

They eating were when, his mother asked him to: Arrives when one other land from, how you treat him?

Mykùra o-suaxàra: Xa senòi aè o-ù arâma ianè irùmo.

Fox replies: I call him eating for us with.

Aramè uaimi o-senoi kunhã mokù, o-iumimi o-ikô uaá.

Then the old-woman calls the young-woman, hidden was who.

Kunhã-moku o-ù-ãn aità irûmo.
The young-woman ate them with.

Mykùra sorib o-ikò, maa-resè kunhã-mokù poranga rête.

Fox content was, because young woman fine very.

Pitùna opè, Mykùra o-só ramè, okèr arâma kunhã mokù irûmo, aè ompù-ãn aè o-nhēē:

Night at, the Fox went when sleep to, the young woman with, she expelled him, she said:

Inti xa-ienõ potàre né irûmo, maa-resè inèma rétè inè.

Not I to sleep will you with, because stinking very much you.

Koêma ramé, uaimi o-mondù ramè kunhã mokú o-iuuka iepea, kunhã moku o-iauáu-ãn.

Morning when, the old woman ordered when the young woman to seek fuel, the young-woman went away....

II

« KUNHÃ MÔKU, URUBU »

« The Young-woman and the Carrion-crow »

O-sŭka mosapŭr pê ôpè, o-só amo rupy;
She arrived three paths at, she went another through;

O-sŭka òka ôpè, o-iñuanti amô uaimi irûmo;
She arrived house at, met other old-woman with;

O-puranû ì-xui: Indè será Inayè sy?
She asked her: You Inaye's mother?

Uáimi o-suaxára: — Ixè aè tenhẽ.
The old-woman replies: I myself yes.

Kunhã mokú o-nhẽẽ: xa ùr aè piri, xa menar arâma aè irûmo.

The young woman said : I come him to, I marry him with.

Uaimi onhẽẽ: Xa só xa iumimi indé, se mbyra poxi reté sesé.

The old-woman said : I go I hide thee, my son creature rude very because.

Koahá uaimi Urubú sy.

This old-woman Carrion-crow's mother.

Karuka ramè, i mbyra o-sŭkà; o-rure xemiára,= itapurú mirīétá, onhẽẽ i sy supè:

Evening when, her son arrived; he brought game, = worms small, he said his mother to :

« *Kusukui pirá mirīta, se sy.* »

«Here is small fish, my mother.»

I sy o-mongaturu ximiára.

His mother tempered the prey.

Aitá o-u-oikó ramè, aè o-puranú:

They eating were when, she asked:

Auá supè o-sŭka waá amô tetâma sui, maá-tá re-monhā i-xupé?

Him to arrives who other land from, how do you him with ?

Urubu o-suaxára : xa senoi aè o-u arâma ianè irûmo.

The Crow replies: I call him eating for us with.

Aramè i sy o-senoi kunkã-moku.

Then his mother called the young-woman.

Urubù sorib-etè an, kunhã-moku poranga retè resè.

The Crow glad very was, young-woman fine very because of.

Pitûna ôpè, aè o-só ramé o-yenõ aè irumo; kunhã-mokú ompú-àn inēma resé aè.

Night at, he went when, to sleep her with; the young-woman expelled him, stinking for his.

Amô koēma ôpè, uaími o-mondù ramè kunhã mokú o-iuuka arama iapeá, kunhã-mokú o-iauau-ãn....

Other morning at, the old-woman ordered when, the young-woman seek to fuel, the young-woman went away....

III

« KUNHÃ-MOKU, INAYÉ »

« The Young-woman and the Sparraw-hawk »

Aè o-sŭka ramè mosapŭr pé ôpè, o-só amõ rupy.

She arrived when three paths at, she went other through.

O-sŭka oka ópè, o-mahẽ yepè uaimi poranga-retè, o-puranú i-xui:—Iné Inayè sy será?

She arrived a house at, saw one old-woman fine very, she asked her: Thou Inaye's mother?

Uaimi o-suaxára: Ixè aè tenhẽ.

Old-woman replies: I myself yes.

Kunhã-moku o-nhẽẽ: xa-ur aé piri xa menar arama aè irumo.

Young-woman said: I come him to, I marry to him with.

Uaimi o-nhẽẽ: xa só xa-iumimi indé; sè mbÿra mira poxî-reté!

Old-woman says: I go I hide thee; my son a *fellow* troublesome very!

Karuka ramè, mbyra o-sŭka; o-rure ximiára, = uira-mirĩ-sétá.

Night at, the son arrived; he brought game, = birds small many.

I sy omon-gaturú uïra mirĩtá aitá oú arãma.

His mother prepared the birds small their eating for.

Aitá oú o-ikó ramè, i sy o-puranu i-xui:

They eating were when, his mother asked him:

Auá supè o-sŭka uaá ramè amô tetãma sui, maã tá re-monhã ixu-pè?

Him to arrives who if other land from, how you do him to?

Inayé o-suaxára: — *Xa senoi aè oú aráma iané irûmo.*

Inayé replied: I call him eating for us with.

Aramè uâimi o-senoi kunhã-moku.

Then the old woman called the young-woman.

Inayè soríb reté, kunhã moku poranga reté resè.

Inayé glad very, the young-woman fine very for.

Aetá o-ker-an iepe-uasú.

They slept together.

Amo ara-ôpé, Urubú o-sŭka Inayè oka ôpé, o-sikari aráma kunhã mokú.

Other day at, the Crow arrived Inayé's house at, looking for the young-woman.

Aità omara-monhã-oan retè kunhã-mokú resè.

They fighted much, the young-woman because of.

Inayè ompúk-ân Urubú akanga.

Inayè brake open the Crow's head.

I sy omo-akú iy, mo-asúk i akanga.

His mother warmed water, washed his head.

Iy sakú reté oân; aaresé i akanga-saua-yma opitá arà opé.....

The water was too warm; therefore his head bald became, since then....................

CHAPTER XIII

CONCLUSION

118.— From all that has been said before, we think, we are enabled to draw the following general conclusions:

(I) That in the Brasilian language all the words are invariable; [27]

(II) That the distinction of number and gender in nouns, adjectives, and pronouns (except the personal) are indicated, either by special words or by postpositions, and other formative elements; [30 to 34, 67 to 69, 74 to 80]

(III) That the persons of verbs are designated by means of prefixes which are, so to say, glued to them, with the same value and signification, as the personal suffixes of the Latin language; [85]

(IV) That the moods and tenses (the Present Indicative excepted) are expressed by the use of special particles, which are placed after the verbal root; [86 to 89]

(v) That, although a noun or an adjective of quality may be used, as a verb, and *vice-versa,* still we find, in general, quite distinct, all the parts of speech, such as : noun, adjective, pronoun, verb, adverb, postposition (prep.), conjunction and interjection; [27, 95, 106]

(vi) That predicative roots are entirely distinct from demonstrative ones, and that they are never confounded in their applications.

(vii) That in derivative or compound-words it is always easy to make the decomposition of the radical and of the formative elements, although there may occur frequent euphonical letters.

— Therefore, we consider these facts and other which were presented before, as a proof, quite sufficient, that the Brasilian speech ought to be rightly classed, as belonging to the family of agglutinative tongues.

CORRIGENDA

Pags.	Ns.	Errata	Corrected
6	3	destinguish	= distinguish
10	6	language sare	= languages are
11	7	indu-ctions	= induc-tions
19	10	knwon	= known
23	12	can, rightly	= can rightly
30	16	the-refore	= there-fore
31	»	gene-ral	= gener-al
38	29	distinguished	= distinguished,
45	38	a s	= an s.
57	57	erciprocally	= reciprocally
59	59	(particle)	= particle)
64	66	to to dig	= to dig
68	69	kunhá	= kunhã
71	71	tventy	= twonty
74	75	that	= that,
80	82	baptised;	= baptised,
81	»	tho those	= those
94	94	so-coll-	= so-call-
»	»	liing	= living
96	96	equal o	= equal to
100	98	a it	= it
103	99	postpo-istions	= postpo-sitions
110	102	t-iné iukd	= t-iné o-iukd
111	103	ixé iukd	= ixé re-iukd
113	104	au-xialiary	= aux-iliary
»	»	verb*stare*	= verb *stare*
121	110	lite-rally	= lit-erally
125	112	lessor-	= lessor.
140	113	violenty	= violently
145	115 (*)	either, or,	= either, or,
»	»	meither	= neither
147	116	$pekoĩ$	= $pekoĩ,$
148	»	pèpè	= pòpè
154	»	yuorselves	= yourselves
157	»	$maã$	= $mahẽ$
159	»	shead	= s head

INDEX

CHAPTER I

CLASSIFICATION OF LANGUAGES.......................... 1
   (1) The monasyllabic period............................ 2
   (2) The agglutinative period........................... 3
   (3) The inflectional period............................ 7
   The study of language................................. 10
   The Bras. lang. and its position...................... 13

CHAPTER II

FHONETIC PRINCIPLES..................................... 19
   Sounds and letters.................................... 22
   Consonants.. 23
   Vowels.. 25
   Diphthongs.. 28
   Table of the alphabetic sounds........................ 29
   Thonetic alterations.................................. 30
   Permutation of sounds................................. 31
   Suppression & addition of letters..................... 33

CHAPTER III

PARTS OF SPEECH.. 36
   Accidence or the forms of words....................... 37
   Gender, number and case............................... 40
   Diminutive and augmentative........................... 43
   Derivation and formation of nouns etc................. 44
   Noun-suffixes... 45
   Agglutination of words................................ 49
   Longer-agglutinative words............................ 55
   Onomatopaic words..................................... 64

CHAPTER IV

ADJECTIVES	65
Accidence of Bras. adjectives	67
Gender and number	68
Comparison	68
Numerals	70
Ordinals	72

CHAPTER V

PRONOUNS	73
Personal pronouns	73
Demonstrative pron.	74
Interrogative pron.	75
Relative pronouns	76
Possessive pron.	76
Indefinite pron.	77

CHAPTER VI

VERBS	79
Voice of verbs	80
Reflexive verbs	81
Transitive verbs	81
Prono. subjects & pers. prefixes	83
Mood	84
Tenses	85
The negation and interrogation	89
Anomalous verbs	90
Remarks	92
Formation of verbs	94
Participles	97

CHAPTER VII

POSTPOSITIONS	97

CHAPTER VIII

ADVERBS..	101
Adverbs of place	101
Adverbs of affirmation, etc, etc.................	103
Adverbs of time...................................	105
Adverbs of manner, quality, etc.................	106

CHAPTER IX

CONJUNCTIONS...	107

CHAPTER X

INTERJECTIONS..	108

CHAPTER XI

MISCELL. RULES & REMARKS............................	109
Syntax of the subject............................	109
Syntax of the object.............................	111
Syntax of the verb...............................	111
The construction of some verbs..................	115
To need and (to) will............................	116
Est meum, est tuum..............................	117
Division of time.................................	118
Salutation or greeting...........................	121
Colours..	121
Review of agglutinative forms...................	122
Original words...................................	132

CHAPTER XII

BRAZILIAN COMPOSITIONS...............................	143
Nhanè Rùba......................................	144
May pituna o-yo-kuáu-an.........................	147
Kunhã mokú o-só uaá &...........................	161

CHAPTER XIII

CONCLUSION...	178

CORRIGENDA...	181

www.ingramcontent.com/pod-product-compliance
Lightning Source LLC
Chambersburg PA
CBHW031440160426
43195CB00010BB/801